# Part 1

# A THEORETICAL INTRODUCTION TO DIVERTICULITIS

It's fascinating to consider that, once upon a time, the human body survived on sheer instinct. Humans naturally adapted to their environments, and so did their bodies. Fast forward to today, and we've adapted to diet trends, shifting from growing our own food to purchasing it from grocery stores. This shift, while incredibly convenient in our fast-paced world, raises questions about dietary issues arising from consuming foods whose components we're often unsure of.

In our modern world, there's a vast array of dietary issues, with diverticulitis being one of the significant gastrointestinal conditions affecting a portion of the population. If you're unfamiliar with this type of inflammation, you're in the right place. This handbook is designed to walk you through all the questions you might have. It will ease you into understanding how to manage diverticulitis, outline measures to look out for, and identify risk factors that can exacerbate the condition. Many people experience digestive issues and struggle to relate them to any specific condition.

This manuscript will teach you how to identify these symptoms and, most importantly, show how lifestyle changes in diet can successfully alleviate symptoms in the acute and flare-up phases. Think of it as your friendly guide to navigating the ins and outs of diverticulitis. We'll take you through everything you need to know, from understanding what this condition is to identifying the risk factors and symptoms. And most importantly, we'll show you how dietary changes can play a crucial role in managing and alleviating those symptoms.

In our world, where little is said about the role of diet in healing the gut, doctors often recommend medication without suggesting natural, holistic practices that can help alleviate symptoms. This book will set out the dietary guides for the three phases of diverticulitis and provide over 81 detailed recipes that you can use every day. The practical part of this book will guide you on which meals to take depending on the stage of your diverticulitis. The meals will be set out to cater to a full day, starting from breakfast, snacks, and main meals.

As we navigate the complexities of modern diets, it's crucial to reflect on how these changes impact our health. This book traverses the evolution of our eating habits, exploring the benefits and challenges of contemporary diets. Join me and uncover how we can balance convenience with mindful eating, ultimately aiming for a healthier, more informed approach to nutrition.

# CHAPTER 1
# Introduction to Diverticulitis

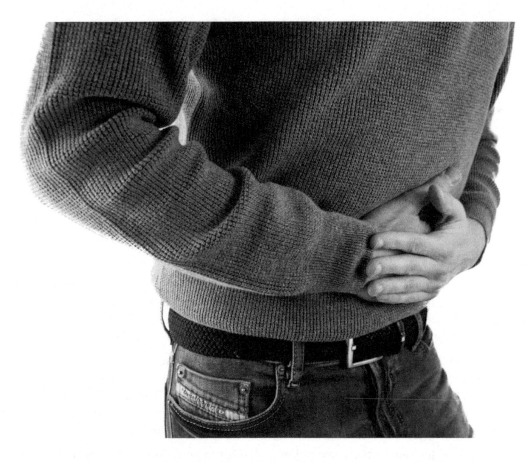

Imagine this: our ancestors once thrived in a world where food was hunted, gathered, and grown with their own hands. The connection between people and their sustenance was direct and intimate. Fast forward to today, and we find ourselves navigating grocery store aisles, reading labels, and wondering about the origins of our food. This evolution in our food habits, while undeniably convenient, has introduced a host of dietary challenges that our ancestors never faced. One of these challenges is diverticulitis, a condition that lurks in the shadows of our modern lifestyle, affecting a significant portion of the population.

In today's fast-paced world, we often overlook the impact of our diet on our overall health, especially when it comes to our gut. Medical professionals tend to prescribe medications as the first line of defense, but there's a growing awareness of the benefits of natural, holistic approaches to health. This chapter aims to bridge that gap by providing a comprehensive guide to how to identify the symptoms of Diverticulitis and manage the condition so that it does not take over your life.

As we journey through this chapter, keep in mind that understanding your body's needs and listening to its signals is paramount. Diverticulitis doesn't have to control your life. With the right knowledge and dietary strategies, you can take charge of your health and enjoy a fulfilling, symptom-free life. So, let's enter this discussion, armed with delicious recipes and practical advice that will empower you to live your best life, even with diverticulitis.

# What is Diverticulitis?

First, let's get to the heart of it: what exactly is diverticulitis? Diverticulitis might sound like a daunting term, but it's simply an inflammation or infection of small pouches called diverticula that can form in your digestive tract. If you're new to this term, don't worry—you're not alone. Many people are unaware of diverticulitis until they experience its uncomfortable symptoms. Think of diverticulitis as those little pouches in your colon getting irritated or infected, leading to pain and discomfort.

According to the National Institute of Diabetes and Digestive and Kidney Diseases (NIDDK), diverticulitis occurs when these pouches form when weak spots in the colon wall give way under pressure. The NIDDK further sets stage for how many people are suffering from this condition, it confirms that about 10% of people over the age of 40 have diverticulosis, a condition that can develop into diverticulitis. This percentage increases to around 50% by the age of 60. Diverticulitis is more common in older adults. (NIDDK, 2021). This doesn't mean that younger people do not suffer from this condition, it only means that reported cases are often of people around the age of 40. If you've developed these symptoms before you turned 40, worry not! We are here to help you walk through the journey of seeking treatment.

# Stages of Diverticulitis

Diverticulitis progresses through three distinct phases: the Flare-Up Phase, Acute Phase, and Remission Phase. Each phase has unique characteristics and requires specific management strategies to ensure effective treatment and long-term health.

**The Flare-Up Phase:** The Flare-Up Phase is marked by the initial onset of symptoms, which are typically triggered by inflammation or infection in the diverticula. Symptoms during this phase can be sudden and intense, causing significant discomfort and include:

- **Symptoms**: Sharp abdominal pain, usually on the lower left side, fever, nausea, constipation or diarrhea.
- **Management**: Rest, hydration, clear liquid diet, over-the-counter pain relievers, antibiotics if prescribed.

During this phase, it is crucial to reduce the strain on the digestive system to allow the inflammation to subside. Avoiding solid foods and consuming clear liquids can help manage symptoms effectively.

**The Acute Phase:** The Acute Phase is when the symptoms of diverticulitis are at their most severe and require immediate medical attention. This phase can lead to serious complications if not treated promptly and include:

- **Symptoms**: Intense abdominal pain, high fever, nausea, vomiting, severe changes in bowel habits, possible complications such as abscesses or perforations.
- **Management**: Hospitalization, intravenous antibiotics, fluids, possible surgery in severe cases.

Prompt and appropriate treatment during the Acute Phase is critical to prevent further complications and ensure the healing of the colon. Hospitalization may be necessary to provide intensive care and monitoring.

**The Remission Phase:** The Remission Phase occurs after the acute symptoms have subsided and the inflammation has reduced. This phase focuses on recovery and preventing future flare-ups and include:

- **Symptoms**: Reduced pain, normal bowel habits, overall improvement in well-being.
- **Management**: Gradual reintroduction of solid foods, high-fiber diet, regular follow-ups with a healthcare provider, lifestyle changes such as increased fiber intake, hydration, and regular exercise.

During remission, individuals should focus on maintaining digestive health through diet and lifestyle modifications. Regular monitoring and follow-up care are essential to ensure long-term health and prevent recurrence of symptoms.

Understanding the phases of diverticulitis is crucial for effective management. By recognizing the symptoms and appropriate treatments for each phase, individuals can take proactive steps to alleviate discomfort, prevent complications, and maintain a healthy digestive system.

# Common Misconceptions

There's a couple of conditions that are often easily mistaken for diverticulitis. Knowing about diverticulitis is crucial. Early detection and treatment can prevent serious complications and improve your quality of life. This also includes lifestyle changes like eating certain kinds of food and engaging in physical exercises which can significantly lower your risk of developing infection.

In the next chapter, we will discuss the known signs and symptoms of diverticulitis in detail. For now it's essential to point out that many people commonly mistake the symptoms of diverticulosis with those of diverticulitis. Understanding the difference between diverticulosis and diverticulitis can help you take proactive steps towards better digestive health. By knowing the symptoms and risk factors, you can seek treatment early and avoid the severe consequences of untreated diverticulitis.

To better understand diverticulitis, let's clarify its relationship with diverticulosis. Diverticulitis stems from a condition called diverticulosis. While diverticulosis involves having these small pouches in your colon and is mostly harmless, diverticulitis is the troublemaker that brings on symptoms and can lead to complications if not treated. In simple terms, diverticulosis is when those small pouches (diverticula) form in the walls of your colon. Most people with diverticulosis don't even know they have it because it usually doesn't cause any symptoms. It's often discovered during routine check-ups or colonoscopies. While diverticulitis is when those pouches become inflamed or infected. Unlike diverticulosis, diverticulitis makes its presence known with symptoms like severe abdominal pain, fever, nausea, and changes in your bowel habits. If not treated, it can lead to serious complications like abscesses, perforations in the colon, and even life-threatening infections.

# Why Understanding Diverticulitis Matters

The confusion between these two conditions often arises because they are part of the same spectrum of disease, and the terms sound similar. However, while diverticulosis is often harmless, diverticulitis requires medical attention and a different approach to treatment.

Understanding the distinction between diverticulosis and diverticulitis is important for several reasons:

1.  **Proper Diagnosis**: Accurate diagnosis is key to managing symptoms effectively. If someone with diverticulosis develops symptoms of diverticulitis, it's crucial to identify this transition to provide appropriate treatment. Misunderstanding the condition can lead to mismanagement, delayed treatment, and potentially serious complications.
2.  **Treatment Approach**: Diverticulosis often doesn't require specific treatment beyond dietary changes, like increasing fiber intake. However, diverticulitis usually needs more intensive treatment, which can include antibiotics, a temporary liquid diet to allow the colon to heal, and in severe cases, surgery. Recognizing the condition accurately ensures that patients receive the right treatment promptly.
3.  **Preventive Measures**: People with diverticulosis can take steps to prevent diverticulitis by maintaining a high-fiber diet, staying hydrated, and exercising regularly. Understanding the risks associated with diverticulosis and knowing how to manage it proactively can reduce the likelihood of developing diverticulitis.
4.  **Monitoring and Follow-Up**: For those diagnosed with diverticulosis, regular follow-ups with a healthcare provider can help monitor the condition and catch any signs of progression to diverticulitis early. Understanding the potential progression from diverticulosis to diverticulitis enables better long-term management and monitoring strategies.
5.  **Education and Awareness**: Educating patients about the differences between diverticulosis and diverticulitis empowers them to recognize symptoms early and seek appropriate medical care. Awareness can also help reduce anxiety and confusion about the condition, leading to better adherence to preventive measures and treatment plans.

Effective management of diverticulitis relies heavily on understanding its relationship with diverticulosis. By recognizing that diverticulosis is typically asymptomatic and harmless, while diverticulitis is an active inflammation requiring medical attention, patients and healthcare providers can work together to ensure timely and appropriate care. This understanding not only helps in treating the acute phases of diverticulitis but also in preventing its occurrence through lifestyle modifications and regular monitoring.

While diverticulosis itself isn't dangerous, it can lead to diverticulitis if those pouches get inflamed or infected. Once you have noticed these signs and are tracking them, you can prevent and manage diverticulitis effectively.

In the following chapters, we'll dive deeper into the causes, symptoms, treatment options, and preventive measures for diverticulitis. This book doesn't just stop at theory—it's also packed with 81 delicious, easy-to-make recipes tailored for those with diverticulitis. These recipes will guide you through all three stages of the disease: the Flare-Up Phase, Acute Phase, and Remission Phase. Our goal is to help you enjoy tasty, satisfying meals while managing your condition effectively. So let's delve into this discussion to better digestive health, one meal at a time.

# CHAPTER 2
# Management and Treatment

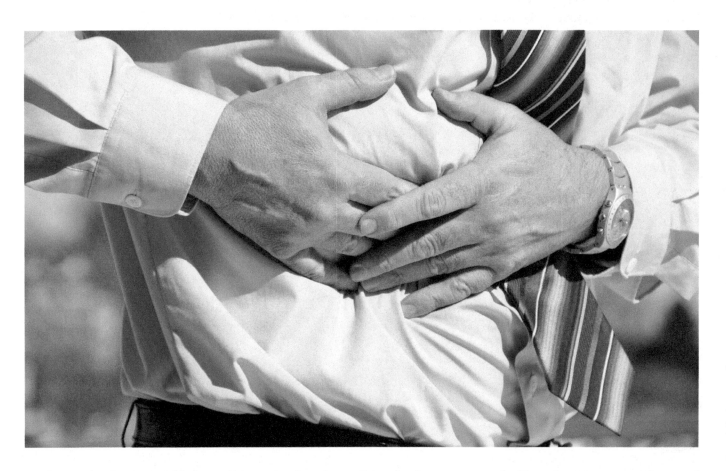

Dealing with a diagnosis of diverticulitis, or any chronic condition for that matter, can be likened to a journey with several stages, much like the stages of grief. Initially, it can feel like mourning the loss of the self-sufficient body you once had, accepting that your body now requires additional care and support. This support might come in various forms, such as medication to manage symptoms or, in more severe cases, surgical procedures to address complications.

The truth is, there is no one-size-fits-all approach to managing a chronic disease. Each person's experience is unique, and what works for one individual might not be effective for another. As patients move past the initial shock of their diagnosis, they enter a phase that requires ongoing support and acceptance. It's essential to learn to live with this new normal, integrating these changes into everyday life without feeling overwhelmed. One of the most significant challenges in dealing with a chronic illness is the continuous nature of the condition. Unlike acute illnesses that come and go, chronic diseases require constant management and vigilance. This ongoing process can be exhausting, both physically and emotionally. Therefore, it's crucial to build a strong support system, comprising healthcare professionals, family, and friends, who can offer encouragement and assistance when needed.

This chapter aims to provide you with the tools and knowledge to adapt to your new circumstances. It offers practical advice and emotional support to help you navigate this transition smoothly. A diagnosis of diverticulitis does not have to stop your life, you can lead a fulfilling life despite the challenges posed by your condition. Remember, you are not alone on this journey. With the right tools and mindset, you can navigate this path with resilience and grace.

When it comes to managing and treating diverticulitis, understanding the available medical treatments and the importance of a proper diet is crucial. Let's dive into the specifics of how doctors recommend treating this condition and how diet plays a pivotal role in both management and prevention.

# Medical Treatment of Diverticulitis

Diverticulitis can range from mild to severe, and the treatment approach varies accordingly. Here's a breakdown of common medical treatments based on the phase of the disease:

## 1. Flare-Up Phase:

During the Flare-Up Phase of diverticulitis, medical treatments are aimed at controlling the infection, managing symptoms, and promoting healing of the inflamed diverticula. Here's an expanded look at the common medical treatments based on this phase:

- **Antibiotics**: When experiencing a mild flare-up, doctors typically prescribe antibiotics to combat the bacterial infection that has caused the inflammation in the diverticula. Antibiotics commonly prescribed include metronidazole, ciprofloxacin, or amoxicillin-clavulanate. These medications work by targeting the bacteria responsible for the infection, reducing their numbers in the colon, and preventing the infection from spreading or worsening. It's crucial to complete the full course of antibiotics as prescribed to ensure effective treatment and reduce the risk of recurrence.
- **Pain Management**: Abdominal pain is a hallmark symptom of diverticulitis during the flare-up phase. To alleviate pain and discomfort, over-the-counter pain relievers such as acetaminophen (Tylenol) are often recommended. It's important to avoid nonsteroidal anti-inflammatory drugs (NSAIDs) like ibuprofen and aspirin during this phase, as they can potentially worsen symptoms and increase the risk of bleeding due to their effect on the gastrointestinal tract.
- **Dietary Modifications**: In the initial stages of a flare-up, a liquid diet is commonly advised to provide rest to the digestive system and allow the inflamed diverticula to heal. Clear liquids such as broth, clear juices, gelatin, and herbal teas are typically recommended during this phase. As symptoms improve, the diet may progress to include low-fiber foods that are gentle on the digestive tract, such as cooked or canned fruits without skins, well-cooked vegetables without seeds, and refined grains like white rice or pasta. The gradual reintroduction of foods helps gauge tolerance and prevent aggravation of symptoms.
- **Rest and Monitoring**: Adequate rest is essential during the flare-up phase to support healing and recovery. Monitoring of symptoms is crucial to assess the effectiveness of treatment and to detect any complications early. It's important to follow up with your healthcare provider as scheduled to ensure that the treatment plan is effective and to make adjustments if needed based on your response to antibiotics and dietary modifications.

These treatment strategies are a major aid to individuals trying to manage the flare-up phase of diverticulitis, promote healing of inflamed diverticula, and reduce the risk of complications. Proper medical guidance and adherence to treatment recommendations play a key role in achieving recovery and preventing recurrence of diverticulitis episodes.

## 2. Acute Phase:

During the Acute Phase of diverticulitis, hospitalization may become necessary if symptoms worsen significantly. Treatment during this critical phase is aimed at aggressively managing the infection and alleviating symptoms to prevent complications:

- **Intravenous Antibiotics**: In cases of severe infection, intravenous (IV) antibiotics are administered to swiftly combat the bacterial infection responsible for the inflammation and potential complications within the diverticula. The use of IV antibiotics ensures rapid delivery and effective absorption into the bloodstream, enhancing their potency and reducing the risk of systemic spread.
- **Hydration**: IV fluids are crucial to maintain adequate hydration levels and electrolyte balance, especially when patients may be unable to consume fluids orally due to the severity of symptoms or the need for bowel rest. Proper hydration supports overall recovery, aids in flushing out toxins, and helps prevent complications associated with dehydration, such as renal dysfunction and electrolyte imbalances.

- **Bowel Rest**: To promote healing and reduce stress on the inflamed bowel, patients are typically placed on a clear liquid diet or maintained on NPO status (nothing by mouth). This approach allows the digestive system to rest, minimizes irritation to the inflamed diverticula, and supports recovery by reducing digestive workload and potential exacerbation of symptoms.
- **Monitoring**: Close monitoring in the hospital setting is essential during the acute phase of diverticulitis. Healthcare providers closely observe vital signs, symptoms, and response to treatment to promptly identify any worsening of infection or development of complications like abscesses or perforations in the colon. Regular monitoring enables timely interventions and adjustments in treatment plans to optimize outcomes and ensure patient safety.

During hospitalization for acute diverticulitis, the coordinated use of IV antibiotics, meticulous hydration management, bowel rest, and vigilant monitoring forms the cornerstone of treatment. This comprehensive approach aims to control infection, alleviate symptoms, and mitigate potential complications, facilitating a faster recovery and reducing the likelihood of disease progression.

**Severe Cases and Complications**:

In severe cases of diverticulitis leading to complications such as abscesses, fistulas, or perforations, surgical intervention becomes necessary to manage and resolve these serious issues. The following surgical options may be considered:

- **Abscess Drainage**: If an abscess develops, it may require drainage to remove the accumulated pus and relieve pressure. This can be done either percutaneously, where a needle is inserted through the skin into the abscess under imaging guidance, or surgically through an open procedure.
- **Resection Surgery**: In cases of recurrent or complicated diverticulitis, surgical resection of the affected segment of the colon may be recommended. This procedure, known as colectomy, involves removing the diseased portion of the colon. Depending on the severity and extent of the disease, colectomy can be performed as a primary resection with immediate reconnection of the remaining parts of the colon (anastomosis). In some cases, especially if the condition is severe or complications are extensive, a two-stage procedure may be necessary. This involves creating a temporary colostomy to divert fecal flow away from the affected area while the colon heals, followed by a subsequent surgery to close the colostomy and restore normal bowel continuity.
- **Emergency Surgery**: In life-threatening situations such as a perforated colon with widespread infection (peritonitis), emergency surgery is essential. The goal of emergency surgery is to repair the perforation in the colon and remove the affected segment to prevent further complications and systemic infection. This procedure requires immediate intervention to stabilize the patient's condition and address the underlying pathology.

Surgical intervention in cases of severe diverticulitis and its complications aims to alleviate symptoms, prevent recurrence, and improve overall outcomes for the patient. The choice of surgical procedure depends on the specific circumstances of the individual case, guided by the extent of the disease, severity of complications, and overall health status of the patient.

# Importance of Diet

Diet plays a crucial role in managing diverticulitis and preventing flare-ups. Here's how you can adapt your diet during different stages of the disease:

## 1. During a Flare-Up:

- **Liquid Diet**: Start with clear liquids such as broth, water, and gelatin to give your colon a rest.
- **Low-Fiber Foods**: Gradually introduce low-fiber foods like white rice, cooked vegetables, and lean proteins. This helps reduce bowel movements and allows the colon to heal.

## 2. Acute Phase Recovery:

- **Gradual Reintroduction of Fiber**: Once symptoms improve, slowly reintroduce fiber into your diet. Start with soluble fiber found in foods like oats, apples, and carrots, as it's gentler on the digestive system.

- **Hydration**: Drinking plenty of water is essential to prevent constipation, especially when increasing fiber intake.

## 3. Remission Phase:

- **High-Fiber Diet**: A diet rich in fiber helps prevent future flare-ups by keeping the stool soft and reducing pressure in the colon. Include foods like whole grains, fruits, vegetables, and legumes.
- **Regular Meals**: Eating regular, balanced meals helps maintain digestive health. Avoid large meals that can strain the digestive system.
- **Probiotics**: Incorporating probiotics, such as yogurt or kefir, can promote a healthy gut microbiome and improve digestion.

# Adapting Your Diet

Managing diverticulitis through diet offers flexibility and adaptability, providing you with the tools to make sustainable dietary changes. Here are practical tips to help you integrate these changes into your daily routine:

1. **Meal Planning**: Planning your meals in advance ensures that you incorporate a diverse range of fiber-rich foods. This approach not only helps you maintain a balanced diet but also reduces the likelihood of opting for less healthy choices when hunger strikes unexpectedly.
2. **Cooking Methods**: Choose cooking methods that are gentle on the digestive system, such as steaming, baking, or poaching. These methods preserve nutrients and minimize the addition of fats that could potentially exacerbate symptoms. Avoid fried foods or dishes heavily seasoned with spices, as these can irritate the colon and worsen symptoms.
3. **Fiber Supplements**: If you find it challenging to meet your fiber needs through food alone, consider incorporating fiber supplements into your daily routine. However, it's essential to consult with your healthcare provider before starting any supplements to ensure they are suitable for your condition and won't interact with any medications you may be taking.
4. **Listen to Your Body**: Every individual's digestive system responds differently to various foods. Pay close attention to how your body reacts after eating different meals. Keeping a food diary can be immensely helpful in identifying trigger foods that may exacerbate symptoms. By tracking your diet and symptoms, you can better understand what works best for your digestive health and make informed choices accordingly.

Remember that consistency and personalized adjustments based on your body's responses are key to maintaining a balanced and supportive diet for managing this condition.

# Making It Fun

Managing diverticulitis doesn't have to be a chore. Here are some fun ways to incorporate a healthy diet into your lifestyle:

1. **Explore Ethnic Cuisines**: Dive into the culinary traditions of different cultures by exploring ethnic cuisines known for their fiber-rich dishes. Mediterranean, Asian, and Latin American cuisines, for example, often feature a variety of vegetables, whole grains, and legumes that can contribute to a balanced diet. Trying out new flavors and cooking styles can keep your meals interesting and nutritious.
2. **Plan Theme Nights**: Spice up your weekly meal planning with themed dinner nights focused on specific dietary goals. For instance, designate a "Meatless Monday" for plant-based meals or a "Fish Friday" for incorporating omega-3-rich fish like salmon or trout. Theme nights add variety and structure to your diet while encouraging you to explore different food options.
3. **Create a Healthy Recipe Collection**: Build a collection of favorite recipes that align with your dietary needs and preferences. Organize them into categories like quick meals, comfort foods, and snacks. Having a repertoire of go-to recipes simplifies meal planning and ensures you always have nutritious options on hand.
4. **Attend Food Festivals and Markets**: Explore local food festivals and farmers' markets to discover fresh, seasonal

produce and artisanal products. These events often showcase a wide range of locally sourced ingredients that can inspire new meal ideas. Engaging with vendors and sampling unique foods can make shopping for nutritious ingredients a pleasurable experience.

5. **Host Potluck Dinners**: Organize potluck dinners with friends or family members who are also interested in healthy eating. Each participant can contribute a dish that aligns with dietary guidelines for diverticulitis. Potluck dinners not only allow you to enjoy a variety of foods but also promote social interaction and support among participants.

6. **Try Food Substitutions**: Experiment with healthier alternatives to traditional ingredients in your favorite recipes. For example, swap refined grains for whole grains like quinoa or brown rice, or use Greek yogurt instead of sour cream in dips and dressings. These substitutions can enhance the nutritional value of your meals without sacrificing taste.

7. **Keep Up with Nutrition Trends**: Stay informed about current nutrition trends and research related to digestive health. Incorporate evidence-based dietary recommendations into your meal planning to optimize your digestive well-being. Being aware of new developments in nutrition can help you make informed choices and adapt your diet as needed.

You don't need to necessarily attempt all activities on the list but you could choose to engage in which one aligns with your personality and hobbies.

# The Bigger Picture

Diet plays a crucial role in managing diverticulitis, but it's also essential to consider the broader aspect of overall health. Implementing additional lifestyle changes can significantly complement your dietary efforts. Regular exercise, for instance, helps keep your digestive system functioning smoothly and can prevent constipation; aim for at least 30 minutes of moderate exercise most days of the week. Stress management is equally important, as stress can negatively impact your digestive health; engaging in stress-reducing activities such as yoga, meditation, or deep breathing exercises can be beneficial. Adequate sleep is another critical factor; ensuring you get enough sleep each night is vital, as lack of sleep can weaken your immune system and increase your risk of infections. Lastly, maintaining regular medical check-ups is essential to monitor your condition and make any necessary adjustments to your treatment plan.

This chapter has reminded us that managing and treating diverticulitis involves a combination of medical treatments and dietary modifications. Remember, it's all about finding a balance that works for you and making sustainable changes that support your overall health. Stay positive, stay informed, and take control of your health journey!

# CHAPTER 3

# Role of Diet in the Management of Diverticulitis

The previous chapter hinted at the benefits of a good diet for patients with diverticulitis. This chapter will provide a detailed explanation of how diets are adjusted during the acute and remission phases. We will delve into what an actual flare-up phase consists of, how to recognize the symptoms that indicate a flare-up, and which foods to avoid or reintroduce. The human body is naturally adaptable to whatever we eat; it responds to both good and bad choices. Our fast-paced lives often lead us to grab the quickest fast foods available. However, there's power in learning about the contents of the food you eat and their nutritional benefits. You don't need to hire an expensive dietician to figure it out; this chapter will help you consciously choose how to eat right.

While this chapter provides an overview of dietary adjustments and the significance of clean eating for managing diverticulitis, it is important to note that the foods mentioned here are not exhaustive. This chapter aims to highlight the importance of mindful eating and offers guidance on what types of foods to include in your diet.

However, for those looking for more specific guidance, including detailed meal plans, Part 2 of this book is dedicated to that very purpose. In Part 2, you will find a variety of meal plans tailored to different stages of the disease, complete with breakfast, lunch, dinner, and snack suggestions. These plans are designed to help you navigate through both the acute and remission phases with ease and confidence.

In the meantime, this chapter serves as an essential foundation, helping you understand the basics of dietary management for diverticulitis. The goal is to make your dietary journey as smooth and effective as possible, offering practical solutions that fit into your lifestyle. It sets the stage for the more detailed and structured guidance you will find later in the book. So, stay tuned and get ready to delve deeper into a diet that supports your health and helps you manage diverticulitis more effectively.

# Diet in Different Stages of the Disease

In the context of managing diverticulitis through diet, it's essential to understand that the human body continuously renews its cells over time. This process, known as cell turnover or cell regeneration, varies across different types of cells in the body. For instance, the cells lining the digestive tract, including the colon affected by diverticulitis, undergo regular renewal to maintain their function and integrity.

Therefore, dietary choices play a crucial role in supporting this physiological process. Nutrient-dense foods rich in vitamins, minerals, and antioxidants provide the building blocks necessary for cell renewal and repair, aiding in the maintenance of a healthy colon lining and overall digestive health. We are all capable of optimizing our body's natural regenerative capabilities and promote long-term wellness given that we follow a good diet plan as per phase of diverticulitis.

The acute phase and remission phase require distinct dietary approaches to ensure the best outcomes. They include the following:

## Acute Phase

During the acute phase of diverticulitis, when symptoms are most severe, your digestive system needs to rest. This means you should consume foods that are easy to digest and unlikely to irritate the inflamed diverticula. Initially, a clear liquid diet is often recommended. These includes:

- **Broths**: Chicken or vegetable broth without any solid pieces.
- **Clear juices**: Apple juice or white grape juice.
- **Gelatin**: Plain gelatin that is free from fruit chunks or other additives.
- **Tea**: Herbal teas without caffeine.

As symptoms improve, you can gradually introduce low-fiber foods. These include:

- **White rice**: Simple and easy to digest.
- **White bread**: Avoid whole grains until symptoms subside.
- **Plain pasta**: Without any heavy sauces or spices.
- **Canned or cooked fruits**: Such as applesauce or canned peaches (without skin).
- **Cooked vegetables**: Like carrots and green beans, well-cooked to ensure they are soft and easy to digest.

## Remission Phase

Once you transition into the remission phase, where symptoms are less pronounced or absent, it's important to gradually reintroduce fiber into your diet. Fiber helps in preventing future flare-ups by promoting regular bowel movements and reducing pressure on the colon. However, it's important to increase fiber intake slowly to avoid triggering symptoms. High-fiber foods to include are:

- **Whole grains**: Brown rice, whole wheat bread, and oatmeal.
- **Fruits**: Fresh fruits with skins, such as apples, pears, and berries.
- **Vegetables**: Raw or lightly cooked vegetables, including leafy greens, carrots, and bell peppers.
- **Legumes**: Beans, lentils, and chickpeas.
- **Nuts and seeds**: In moderation, as they are good sources of fiber and healthy fats.

# Foods to Avoid and Prefer

Knowing which foods to avoid during a flare-up and which to reintroduce gradually is key to managing diverticulitis effectively. Here's a guide to help you navigate this process.

## Foods to Avoid During a Flare-Up

During a flare-up, certain foods can exacerbate symptoms and should be avoided. These include:

- **High-fiber foods**: Whole grains, raw fruits, and vegetables.
- **Seeds and nuts**: These can be difficult to digest and may irritate the colon.
- **Popcorn**: The kernels can be problematic for inflamed diverticula.
- **Spicy foods**: These can irritate the digestive tract and worsen symptoms.
- **Fatty foods**: Fried foods and high-fat dairy products can be hard to digest.
- **Caffeinated beverages**: Coffee and certain teas can increase bowel activity and cause discomfort.

## Foods to Gradually Reintroduce

Once you are in the remission phase, you can start reintroducing more nutritious foods that support overall health and help maintain digestive regularity. These foods include:

- **High-fiber fruits**: Apples, berries, and pears (with skins on).
- **Vegetables**: Broccoli, carrots, and spinach.
- **Whole grains**: Brown rice, quinoa, and whole wheat bread.
- **Legumes**: Beans, lentils, and peas.
- **Nuts and seeds**: Chia seeds, flaxseeds, and almonds (in moderation).
- **Lean proteins**: Chicken, fish, and tofu.

# The Power of a Proper Diet

Adopting a proper diet is not just about avoiding certain foods during flare-ups; it's about embracing a lifestyle that promotes overall well-being and prevents future episodes. A diet rich in whole foods, fibers, and lean proteins can significantly impact your digestive health.

## Practical Tips for a Diverticulitis-Friendly Diet

- **Stay Hydrated**: Drinking plenty of water helps to soften stool and promote regular bowel movements. Aim for at least eight glasses of water a day.
- **Eat Small, Frequent Meals**: This helps to ease the digestive process and reduce the burden on your colon.
- **Chew Thoroughly**: Breaking down food thoroughly in your mouth aids digestion and reduces the risk of irritating your intestines.
- **Exercise Regularly**: Physical activity promotes bowel regularity and overall health.
- **Listen to Your Body**: Pay attention to how your body responds to different foods and adjust your diet accordingly.

Adapting your diet during the different stages of diverticulitis is essential for managing symptoms and promoting long-term health. Note that, you don't need to overhaul your diet overnight. Small, consistent changes can make a significant difference. Embrace the journey to better health with patience and mindfulness, and your body will thank you.

# CHAPTER 4
# Dietary Guides for the 3 Phases of Diverticulitis

Dealing with diverticulitis means navigating through different phases, each demanding its own set of dietary strategies to manage symptoms and promote healing. Let's dive into what to eat (and what to avoid) during each phase—Flare-Up, Acute, and Remission—to help you stay on track and feel your best.

## Flare up Phase

During the flare-up phase of diverticulitis, individuals experience heightened inflammation and irritation of the diverticula in the colon. This phase is characterized by intense abdominal pain, fever, nausea, and changes in bowel habits such as diarrhea or constipation. Managing symptoms effectively during this acute period is crucial to prevent complications and promote healing.

### Importance of a Clear Liquid Diet

A clear liquid diet is often recommended during the flare-up phase of diverticulitis. This dietary approach helps to rest the digestive system by providing easily digestible nutrients while minimizing irritation to inflamed areas in the colon. Clear liquids are defined as liquids that are clear and transparent, allowing for easy absorption and minimal strain on the digestive tract.

**Benefits of a Clear Liquid Diet**:

- **Reduces Digestive Workload**: Clear liquids require minimal digestion, allowing the intestines to rest and heal.
- **Provides Hydration**: Many clear liquids are hydrating, helping to maintain fluid balance and prevent dehydration, which is crucial during illness.
- **Minimizes Irritation**: Since clear liquids contain no solid particles or fiber, they do not aggravate inflamed diverticula, helping to alleviate pain and discomfort.

## Table of Foods to Avoid and Recommended Foods

| FOODS TO AVOID | RECOMMENDED FOODS |
| --- | --- |
| Spicy foods (e.g., chili peppers, hot sauce) | Clear broth (vegetable, chicken, fish or beef) |
| Fried foods (e.g., French fries, fried chicken) | Clear fruit juices (without pulp, pear juice, white cranberry juice) |
| Dairy products (e.g., milk, cheese) | Clear vegetable juices (strained) |
| Processed sugars | Plain gelatin (without fruit pieces) |
| Whole grains (e.g., whole wheat, barley) | Ice pops (without fruit pieces) |
| Nuts and seeds (e.g., almonds, sunflower seeds) | Clear electrolyte drinks (like sports drinks) |
| Beans and legumes (e.g., kidney beans, lentils) | Herbal teas (non-caffeinated, non-spicy, chamomile |
| Carbonated beverages (e.g., soda, sparkling water) | Plain water (still or sparkling) |
| Alcohol (e.g., beer, wine) | Fruit-flavored sorbets (without fruit pieces) |

# Acute Phase

The acute phase of diverticulitis marks a period of active inflammation and irritation of the diverticula in the colon. During this phase, individuals often experience intensified symptoms such as severe abdominal pain, fever, nausea, and changes in bowel habits. Managing the acute phase effectively is crucial to alleviate discomfort, prevent complications like abscess formation or perforation, and promote healing of the inflamed intestinal tissues.

## Importance of a Low-Residue Diet

A low-residue diet is recommended during the acute phase of diverticulitis to minimize intestinal irritation and reduce the workload on the digestive system. Residue refers to indigestible parts of food, including fiber, which can be rough on inflamed diverticula. By opting for foods that are easily digestible and low in fiber, individuals can help to soothe the intestines and allow them to heal without additional strain.

**Benefits of a Low-Residue Diet**:

1. **Reduces Bowel Movements**: Low-residue foods produce less waste and bulk in the intestines, which can help to decrease frequency and urgency of bowel movements.
2. **Minimizes Irritation**: Foods low in fiber are gentler on inflamed diverticula, reducing the risk of exacerbating symptoms like abdominal pain and bloating.
3. **Supports Healing**: By easing the digestive process, a low-residue diet supports the healing of inflamed intestinal tissues and promotes recovery from acute diverticulitis.

## Table of Recommended Foods and Foods to be Avoided

| FOODS TO AVOID | RECOMMENDED FOODS |
|---|---|
| Whole grain bread and cereals (e.g., whole wheat bread, bran flakes) | White bread (without seeds) |
| Raw fruits (especially with skins and seeds) (e.g., apples, berries) | White rice |
| Raw vegetables (especially with skins and seeds) (e.g., broccoli, bell peppers) | Pasta (without whole grains) |
| Nuts and seeds (e.g., almonds, chia seeds) | Clear soups (strained and low-sodium) |
| Beans and legumes (e.g., chickpeas, black beans) | Smooth nut butters (e.g., smooth peanut butter) |
| Tough meats (e.g., steak,lamb chops) | Dairy substitutes (like almond milk or lactose-free products) |
| Fried foods (e.g., fried chicken, French fries) | Eggs (well-cooked) |
| Processed sugars | Lean tender meats (like poultry or fish) |
| Spicy foods (e.g., hot peppers, curry) | Canned or cooked fruits (without skins or seeds) |
| Carbonated beverages (e.g., soda, sparkling water) | Cooked vegetables (peeled and well-cooked) |

# Remission Phase

Welcome to the remission phase—where we're slowly reintroducing fiber back into your diet like welcoming an old friend. This phase focuses on maintaining digestive health and preventing future flare-ups. The remission phase of diverticulitis follows the acute phase and is characterized by a period of reduced symptoms or symptom-free intervals. During this phase, the focus shifts towards gradually reintroducing fiber into the diet to support optimal intestinal health and prevent future flare-ups. This phase is crucial for long-term management and involves making dietary adjustments to maintain digestive wellness.

### Gradual Reintroduction of Fiber

In the remission phase, the gradual reintroduction of fiber plays a pivotal role in promoting digestive health. Fiber adds bulk to stool, which helps to regulate bowel movements and prevents constipation. It also supports the growth of beneficial gut bacteria and maintains the integrity of the intestinal lining. However, reintroducing fiber too quickly or consuming high-fiber foods that are difficult to digest can potentially trigger symptoms in individuals with diverticulitis. Therefore, a cautious approach is recommended.

**Benefits of Gradual Fiber Reintroduction**:

1. **Improved Bowel Regularity**: Fiber helps to promote regular and healthy bowel movements, reducing the risk of constipation or diarrhea.
2. **Enhanced Gut Health**: Fiber-rich foods support the growth of beneficial bacteria in the gut, which contribute to overall digestive wellness.
3. **Reduced Risk of Flare-ups**: By maintaining bowel regularity and intestinal health, gradual fiber reintroduction may help to reduce the likelihood of diverticulitis flare-ups.

## Table of Recommended Foods and Foods to Avoid

| FOODS TO AVOID | RECOMMENDED FOODS |
|---|---|
| Spicy Foods: Hot peppers, chili powder, and other spicy seasonings that can irritate the digestive tract. | Cooked Vegetables: Soft-cooked or steamed vegetables such as carrots, spinach, zucchini, squash, sweet potatoes, and green beans. |
| Fatty Foods: High-fat dairy products, fried foods, creamy sauces, and fatty cuts of meat that may be difficult to digest. | Fruits (without skins): Soft fruits that are peeled or cooked, such as bananas, melons (like cantaloupe or honeydew), applesauce, cooked pears, and berries. |
| Processed Foods: Foods high in refined sugars, artificial additives, and preservatives that may disrupt digestive function. | Well-Cooked Whole Grains: Whole grains that are well-cooked and easily digestible, including brown rice, quinoa, oatmeal, couscous, and cream of wheat. |
| Excessively High-Fiber Foods: While fiber is important, consuming large quantities of high-fiber foods suddenly can overwhelm the digestive system. | Legumes: Beans, lentils, chickpeas, and split peas cooked until soft and well-mashed or blended into soups and stews. |
| Alcohol and Caffeine: These substances can stimulate the intestines and potentially exacerbate symptoms in some individuals. | Lean Proteins: Tender meats such as chicken breast, turkey, lean cuts of beef, fish (like salmon or cod), and eggs prepared without added fats. |
| | Low-Fat Dairy: Plain yogurt, kefir, and small amounts of mild cheeses like mozzarella or cottage cheese. |
| | 1.     Nuts and Seeds (in moderation): Soft nuts and seeds such as almond butter, smooth nut butters, ground flaxseeds, and pumpkin seeds. |
| | Healthy Oils: Olive oil, avocado oil, and flaxseed oil used sparingly for cooking or as dressings. |

**Part 2**

# RECIPE BOOK

## Navigating Your Diverticulitis Diet: A Fun and Tasty Guide

We've all been at that point where we need to make changes to our diet but feel overwhelmed by the options and unsure where to start. If you're dealing with diverticulitis, this can be even more challenging. But don't worry – this section is here to guide you through it all with ease and enjoyment.

Now that we've covered the ins and outs of diverticulitis, it's time to dive into the fun part – the food! This section is your go-to guide for what to eat at each stage of your diverticulitis journey. Whether you're dealing with a flare-up, in the acute phase, or happily cruising in remission, we've got delicious meals tailored just for you.

As you navigate the different meals in this section, relate all the information to what we discussed in Part One of the book. You should already know the signs and symptoms that indicate which phase of inflammation you are in. This section has the meal recipes separated by phase: the flare-up phase, acute phase, and remission phase.

Each meal plan is designed to cater to a full day's worth of eating, from breakfast to snacks and main meals. We'll help you understand which foods to embrace and which to avoid during each phase, making it easier for you to navigate your dietary choices with confidence.

We'll start by recapping the key points from the first part of the book, ensuring you're equipped with the necessary knowledge to identify the phase of inflammation you're in. From there, we'll dive into the specifics of each phase, providing clear and practical meal plans that align with your body's needs. No more guessing games—just straightforward guidance to help you manage your condition effectively.

# Understanding Your Phase

Before we get cooking, it's essential to understand which phase you're in. Part 1 of this book gave you all the clues to identify your symptoms and pinpoint your current stage. Now, let's match those phases with the right meals.

## The Flare-Up Phase

When you're in the flare-up phase, your digestive system needs a break. Think of it as a spa day for your gut – lots of rest and gentle care. The meals in this section are designed to soothe your system and provide essential nutrients without overloading your digestive tract. You'll find recipes that are bland, easy to digest, and low in fiber, giving your gut the rest it needs to start healing.

## The Acute Phase

In the acute phase, your gut is starting to heal, but it still needs gentle, low-fiber foods. Here, you can begin to reintroduce more variety into your diet while still being careful. The recipes in this section offer a bit more flavor and substance, yet remain easy on your digestive system. Think of it as slowly waking your gut up with gentle stretches before diving back into more intense activity.

## The Remission Phase

In the remission phase, you can gradually reintroduce more fiber into your diet. This is the time to enjoy a variety of foods while still being mindful of your digestive health. The recipes here are designed to help you rebuild and maintain your health with delicious, nutrient-rich meals that include a balance of fiber, protein, and healthy fats. You'll find dishes that are satisfying and full of flavor, allowing you to enjoy your food without worry.

## Ready, Set, Cook!

By following these tailored meal plans, you'll support your digestive health at every stage of your diverticulitis journey. Remember, each phase has specific dietary needs, and these meals are designed to help you manage your condition while enjoying delicious food. So, grab your apron and get ready to cook your way to better health!

Welcome to a new way of eating – one that celebrates abundance, flavor, and nourishment. Let's get started on this culinary journey to better health and happier eating!

*N.B- 1) For any recipes within this book that call for the use of broths, readers are advised to consult the "**Clear Broths and Soups**" section under the "**Acute Phase**" recipes. This section provides detailed guidance and specific recipes to ensure that the broths used are appropriate and align with the dietary recommendations presented in this book. Please refer to that section for comprehensive instructions and ingredient lists to prepare the necessary broths. **2)** All bacon cuts refer to beef, chicken, and turkey cuts. Pork, by and large, increases inflammation and is not a recommended food for people suffering from diverticulitis.*

## Flare-Up Phase

## Breakfast

# Clear Chicken Broth

| Preparation Time | Cooking Time | Total Time | Difficulty |
|---|---|---|---|
| 5 minutes | 15 minutes | 20 minutes | Easy |

**Servings**
1 person (For more people, multiply the ingredients by the number of people)

### INGREDIENTS:
- 1 cup clear chicken broth (fat-free and without solid pieces)
- English Touch: A splash of lemon juice
- American Touch: Bay leaf during cooking

### PROCEDURE:
2. In a small pot, bring the chicken broth to a boil.
3. Add a splash of lemon juice (if using the English touch) or a bay leaf (if using the American touch).
4. Reduce heat and simmer for 15 minutes.
5. Remove the bay leaf if used.
6. Serve warm.

### NUTRITIONAL VALUES:
- Calories: 15
- Carbohydrates: 0g
- Proteins: 3g
- Fats: 0g
- Fiber: 0g
- Sodium: 500mg
- Glucose: 0g
- Cholesterol: 0mg

### SUGGESTED SUBSTITUTIONS:
- For lemon juice, you can use a splash of lime juice.
- For the bay leaf, you can use a sprig of thyme.

# Sugar-Free Gelatin

| Preparation Time | Cooking Time | Total Time | Difficulty |
|---|---|---|---|
| 5 minutes | 2 hours (chilling time) | 2 hours 5 minutes | Easy |

**Servings**
1 person (For more people, multiply the ingredients by the number of people)

## INGREDIENTS:
- 1 cup sugar-free gelatin (any clear flavor)
- English Touch: Sprig of mint
- American Touch: Lemon slice

## PROCEDURE:
1. Prepare the gelatin according to the package instructions.
2. Pour the gelatin mixture into a serving dish.
3. Chill in the refrigerator for 2 hours or until set.
4. Garnish with a sprig of mint or a lemon slice before serving.

## NUTRITIONAL VALUES (PER SERVING):
- Calories: 10
- Carbohydrates: 0g
- Proteins: 2g
- Fats: 0g
- Fiber: 0g
- Sodium: 45mg
- Glucose: 0g
- Cholesterol: 0mg

## SUGGESTED SUBSTITUTIONS:
- For mint, you can use a basil leaf.
- For lemon slices, you can use an orange slice.

# Clear Vegetable Broth

| Preparation Time | Cooking Time | Total Time | Difficulty |
|---|---|---|---|
| 10 minutes | 45 minutes | 55 minutes | Easy |

**Servings**
1 person (For more people, multiply the ingredients by the number of people)

## INGREDIENTS:
- 1 cup clear vegetable broth (fat-free and without solid pieces)
- English Touch: Slice of fresh ginger during cooking
- American Touch: Pinch of sea salt

## PROCEDURE:
1. In a pot, bring the vegetable broth to a boil.
2. Add the slice of fresh ginger.
3. Reduce heat and simmer for 45 minutes.
4. Remove the ginger slice.
5. Season with a pinch of sea salt.
6. Serve warm.

## NUTRITIONAL VALUES (PER SERVING):
- Calories: 30
- Carbohydrates: 7g
- Proteins: 1g
- Fats: 0g
- Fiber: 2g
- Sodium: 50mg
- Glucose: 3g
- Cholesterol: 0mg

## SUGGESTED SUBSTITUTIONS:
- For fresh ginger, you can use a garlic clove.
- For sea salt, you can use Himalayan salt.

# Weak Green Tea

| Preparation Time | Cooking Time | Total Time | Difficulty |
|---|---|---|---|
| 5 minutes | 5 minutes | 10 minutes | Easy |

**Servings**
1 person (For more people, multiply the ingredients by the number of people)

## INGREDIENTS:
- 1 cup weak green tea
- English Touch: Fresh mint leaf
- American Touch: Lemon slice

## PROCEDURE:
1. Brew green tea using one tea bag or 1 tsp of loose leaves in hot water for 2-3 minutes.
2. Remove the tea bag or strain the loose leaves.
3. Add a fresh mint leaf or a lemon slice according to preference.
4. Serve warm.

## NUTRITIONAL VALUES:
- Calories: 2
- Carbohydrates: 0g
- Proteins: 0g
- Fats: 0g
- Fiber: 0g
- Sodium: 0mg
- Glucose: 0g
- Cholesterol: 0mg

## SUGGESTED SUBSTITUTIONS:
- For fresh mint leaves, you can use a basil leaf.
- For lemon slices, you can use a lime slice.

# Rice Water

| Preparation Time | Cooking Time | Total Time | Difficulty |
|---|---|---|---|
| 10 minutes | 20 minutes | 30 minutes | Easy |

**Servings**
1 person (For more people, multiply the ingredients by the number of people)

## INGREDIENTS:
- 4 cups water (32 fl oz or 950 ml)
- 1/2 cup rice (3.5 oz or 100 g)
- English Touch: A splash of lemon juice
- American Touch: Small amount of honey

## PROCEDURE:
1. In a large pot, bring the water to a boil.
2. Add the rice and reduce the heat to a simmer for 20 minutes.
3. Strain the rice, reserving the liquid.
4. Add a splash of lemon juice or a small amount of honey as desired.
5. Serve warm or chilled.

## NUTRITIONAL VALUES:
- Calories: 20
- Carbohydrates: 5g
- Proteins: 0g
- Fats: 0g
- Fiber: 0g
- Sodium: 5mg
- Glucose: 0g
- Cholesterol: 0mg

## SUGGESTED SUBSTITUTIONS:
- For lemon juice, you can use lime juice.
- For honey, you can use a small amount of maple syrup.

# Snacks

## Coconut Water

| Preparation Time | Cooking Time | Total Time | Difficulty |
|---|---|---|---|
| 5 minutes | 0 minutes | 5 minutes | Easy |

**Servings**
1 person (For more people, multiply the ingredients by the number of people)

### INGREDIENTS:
- 1 cup coconut water (8 fl oz or 240 ml)
- English Touch: Add a splash of lime
- American Touch: Add an orange slice

### PROCEDURE:
1. Pour the coconut water into a glass.
2. Add a splash of lime juice for an English touch.
3. Add an orange slice for an American touch.
4. Serve chilled.

### NUTRITIONAL VALUES:
- Calories: 45
- Carbohydrates: 11g
- Proteins: 0g
- Fats: 0g
- Fiber: 0g
- Sodium: 25mg
- Glucose: 10g
- Cholesterol: 0mg

### SUGGESTED SUBSTITUTIONS:
- For lime juice, you can use lemon juice.
- For an orange slice, you can use a grapefruit slice.

## Clear Beef Broth

| Preparation Time | Cooking Time | Total Time | Difficulty |
|---|---|---|---|
| 10 minutes | 45 minutes | 55 minutes | Easy |

**Servings**
1 person (For more people, multiply the ingredients by the number of people)

### INGREDIENTS:
- 1 cup clear beef broth (fat-free and without solid pieces)
- English Touch: Add a fresh thyme leaf
- American Touch: Add a pinch of black pepper

### PROCEDURE:
1. Pour the clear beef broth into a pot.
2. Add the fresh thyme leaf for the English touch.
3. Add a pinch of black pepper for the American touch.
4. Heat the broth over medium heat until it simmers.
5. Serve warm.

### NUTRITIONAL VALUES:
- Calories: 15
- Carbohydrates: 0g
- Proteins: 3g
- Fats: 0g
- Fiber: 0g
- Sodium: 300mg
- Glucose: 0g
- Cholesterol: 0mg

### SUGGESTED SUBSTITUTIONS:
- For thyme leaf, you can use rosemary.
- For black pepper, you can use white pepper.

# White Cranberry Juice

| Preparation Time | Cooking Time | Total Time | Difficulty |
|---|---|---|---|
| 5 minutes | 0 minutes | 5 minutes | Easy |

**Servings**
1 person (For more people, multiply the ingredients by the number of people)

## INGREDIENTS:

- 1 cup white cranberry juice (without pulp)
- English Touch: Add a mint leaf
- American Touch: Add a lemon slice

## PROCEDURE:

1. Pour the white cranberry juice into a glass.
2. For the English touch, add a fresh mint leaf.
3. For the American touch, add a lemon slice.
4. Serve chilled.

## NUTRITIONAL VALUES:

- Calories: 120
- Carbohydrates: 30g
- Proteins: 0g
- Fats: 0g
- Fiber: 0g
- Sodium: 5mg
- Glucose: 28g
- Cholesterol: 0mg

## SUGGESTED SUBSTITUTIONS:

- For mint leaves, you can use basil.
- For lemon slices, you can use lime slices.

# Clear Vegetable Broth

| Preparation Time | Cooking Time | Total Time | Difficulty |
|---|---|---|---|
| 10 minutes | 45 minutes | 55 minutes | Easy |

**Servings**
1 person (For more people, multiply the ingredients by the number of people)

## INGREDIENTS:

- 1 cup clear vegetable broth (fat-free and without solid pieces)
- English Touch: Add a bay leaf during cooking
- American Touch: Add a pinch of sweet paprika

## PROCEDURE:

1. In a small pot, heat the clear vegetable broth.
2. For the English touch, add a bay leaf during cooking and simmer for a few minutes.
3. For the American touch, add a pinch of sweet paprika.
4. Serve warm.

## NUTRITIONAL VALUES:

- Calories: 10
- Carbohydrates: 2g
- Proteins: 0g
- Fats: 0g
- Fiber: 0g
- Sodium: 20mg
- Glucose: 1g
- Cholesterol: 0mg

## SUGGESTED SUBSTITUTIONS:

- For bay leaves, you can use a sprig of fresh thyme.
- For sweet paprika, you can use a dash of cayenne pepper.

# Pear Juice

| Preparation Time | Cooking Time | Total Time | Difficulty |
|---|---|---|---|
| 5 minutes | 0 minutes | 5 minutes | Easy |

**Servings**
2 people

## INGREDIENTS:
- 2 cups pear juice without pulp (16 fl oz or 475 ml)
- English Touch: Add 2 sprigs of rosemary (2 sprigs or 6 g)
- American Touch: Add a pinch of cinnamon (1/8 tsp or 0.3 g)

## PROCEDURE:
1. Pour the pear juice into a serving pitcher.
2. For an English touch, add the sprigs of rosemary and let it infuse for 2-3 minutes. Remove the rosemary before serving.
3. For an American touch, add the pinch of cinnamon and stir well.
4. Serve the juice chilled or at room temperature.

## NUTRITIONAL VALUES (PER SERVING):
- **Calories:** 110
- **Carbohydrates:** 28g
- **Proteins:** 0g
- **Fats:** 0g
- **Fiber:** 0g
- **Sodium:** 10mg
- **Glucose:** 22g
- **Cholesterol:** 0mg

## SUGGESTED SUBSTITUTIONS:
- For rosemary, you can use a sprig of mint.
- For cinnamon, you can use a pinch of nutmeg.

# Chamomile Tea

| Preparation Time | Cooking Time | Total Time | Difficulty |
|---|---|---|---|
| 5 minutes | 5 minutes | 10 minutes | Easy |

**Servings**
2 people

## INGREDIENTS:
- 2 cups unsweetened chamomile tea (16 fl oz or 475 ml)
- English Touch: Add a splash of lime juice (2 tsp or 10 ml)
- American Touch: Add a drop of vanilla extract (1/8 tsp or 0.6 ml)

## PROCEDURE:
1. Brew the chamomile tea according to package instructions.
2. For an English touch, add the splash of lime juice and stir.
3. For an American touch, add the drop of vanilla extract and stir.
4. Serve the tea warm or chilled.

## NUTRITIONAL VALUES (PER SERVING):
- **Calories:** 0
- **Carbohydrates:** 0g
- **Proteins:** 0g
- **Fats:** 0g
- **Fiber:** 0g
- **Sodium:** 0mg
- **Glucose:** 0g
- **Cholesterol:** 0mg

## SUGGESTED SUBSTITUTIONS:
- For chamomile tea, you can use peppermint tea.
- For lime juice, you can use lemon juice.
- For vanilla extract, you can use a pinch of ground cinnamon.

# Clear Fish Broth

| Preparation Time | Cooking Time | Total Time | Difficulty |
|---|---|---|---|
| 10 minutes | 30 minutes | 40 minutes | Easy |

**Servings**
2 people

## INGREDIENTS:

- 2 cups clear fish broth (fat-free and without solid pieces) (16 fl oz or 475 ml)
- English Touch: Add a lemon slice during cooking (1 slice or 10 g)
- American Touch: Add a pinch of Herbes de Provence (1/8 tsp or 0.2 g)

## PROCEDURE:

1. In a large pot, bring the clear fish broth to a boil.
2. For an English touch, add the lemon slice during cooking and simmer for 30 minutes. Remove the lemon slice before serving.
3. For an American touch, add the pinch of Herbes de Provence and stir well. Simmer for 30 minutes.
4. Serve the broth warm.

## NUTRITIONAL VALUES (PER SERVING):

- **Calories:** 10
- **Carbohydrates:** 0g
- **Proteins:** 2g
- **Fats:** 0g
- **Fiber:** 0g
- **Sodium:** 200mg
- **Glucose:** 0g
- **Cholesterol:** 0mg

## SUGGESTED SUBSTITUTIONS:

- For lemon slice, you can use a slice of lime.
- For Herbes de Provence, you can use a pinch of Italian seasoning.

# Clear Chicken Soup

| Preparation Time | Cooking Time | Total Time | Difficulty |
|---|---|---|---|
| 10 minutes | 45 minutes | 55 minutes | Easy |

**Servings**
1 person (For more people, multiply the ingredients by the number of people)

## INGREDIENTS:
- 4 cups water (32 fl oz or 950 ml)
- 1 medium carrot, peeled and chopped (1/2 lb or 225 g)
- 1 stalk celery, chopped (1/4 lb or 115 g)
- 1 bunch fresh parsley (1 oz or 30 g)
- 1 bay leaf (1 leaf or 1 g)
- 1 cup clear chicken broth (fat-free and without solid pieces)
- English Touch: a splash of lemon juice
- American Touch: a bay leaf during cooking

## NUTRITIONAL VALUES:
- Calories: 30
- Carbohydrates: 7g
- Proteins: 1g
- Fats: 0g
- Fiber: 2g
- Sodium: 50mg
- Glucose: 3g
- Cholesterol: 0mg

## PROCEDURE:
1. In a large pot, bring the water to a boil.
2. Add the carrot, celery, parsley, and bay leaf.
3. Reduce heat and simmer for 45 minutes.
4. Strain the broth, discarding the solids.
5. Add the clear chicken broth to the strained vegetable broth.
6. For the English Touch, add a splash of lemon juice.
7. For the American Touch, add a bay leaf during cooking.
8. Serve warm.

## SUGGESTED SUBSTITUTIONS:
- For parsley, you can use cilantro.
- For bay leaves, you can use thyme.

# Carrot Cream Soup

| Preparation Time | Cooking Time | Total Time | Difficulty |
|---|---|---|---|
| 10 minutes | 45 minutes | 55 minutes | Easy |

**Servings**
1 person (For more people, multiply the ingredients by the number of people)

## INGREDIENTS:
- 4 cups water (32 fl oz or 950 ml)
- 1 medium carrot, peeled and chopped (1/2 lb or 225 g)
- 1 stalk celery, chopped (1/4 lb or 115 g)
- 1 bunch fresh parsley (1 oz or 30 g)
- 1 bay leaf (1 leaf or 1 g)
- 1 cup carrot cream (cooked carrots blended with clear broth)
- English Touch: a parsley leaf
- American Touch: a pinch of paprika

## PROCEDURE:
1. In a large pot, bring the water to a boil.
2. Add the carrot, celery, parsley, and bay leaf.
3. Reduce heat and simmer for 45 minutes.
4. Strain the broth, discarding the solids.
5. In a blender, combine the cooked carrots from the broth with 1 cup of the clear broth and blend until smooth to create the carrot cream.
6. Add the carrot cream back into the pot with the clear broth.
7. For the English Touch, add a parsley leaf as garnish.
8. For the American Touch, add a pinch of paprika to the soup.
9. Serve warm.

## NUTRITIONAL VALUES:
- Calories: 30
- Carbohydrates: 7g
- Proteins: 1g
- Fats: 0g
- Fiber: 2g
- Sodium: 50mg
- Glucose: 3g
- Cholesterol: 0mg

## SUGGESTED SUBSTITUTIONS:
- For parsley, you can use cilantro.
- For bay leaves, you can use thyme.

# Clear Beef Broth

| Preparation Time | Cooking Time | Total Time | Difficulty |
|---|---|---|---|
| 10 minutes | 45 minutes | 55 minutes | Easy |

**Servings**
1 person (For more people, multiply the ingredients by the number of people)

## INGREDIENTS:

- 4 cups water (32 fl oz or 950 ml)
- 1 medium carrot, peeled and chopped (1/2 lb or 225 g)
- 1 stalk celery, chopped (1/4 lb or 115 g)
- 1 bunch fresh parsley (1 oz or 30 g)
- 1 bay leaf (1 leaf or 1 g)
- 1 cup clear beef broth (fat-free and without solid pieces)
- English Touch: a fresh thyme leaf
- American Touch: a pinch of black pepper

## PROCEDURE:

1. In a large pot, bring the water to a boil.
2. Add the carrot, celery, parsley, and bay leaf.
3. Reduce heat and simmer for 45 minutes.
4. Strain the broth, discarding the solids.
5. Add the clear beef broth to the strained vegetable broth.
6. For the English Touch, add a fresh thyme leaf.
7. For the American Touch, add a pinch of black pepper.
8. Serve warm.

## NUTRITIONAL VALUES:

- Calories: 30
- Carbohydrates: 7g
- Proteins: 1g
- Fats: 0g
- Fiber: 2g
- Sodium: 50mg
- Glucose: 3g
- Cholesterol: 0mg

## SUGGESTED SUBSTITUTIONS:

- For parsley, you can use cilantro.
- For bay leaves, you can use thyme.

# Zucchini Cream Soup

| Preparation Time | Cooking Time | Total Time | Difficulty |
|---|---|---|---|
| 10 minutes | 45 minutes | 55 minutes | Easy |

**Servings**
1 person (For more people, multiply the ingredients by the number of people)

## INGREDIENTS:

- 4 cups water (32 fl oz or 950 ml)
- 1 medium carrot, peeled and chopped (1/2 lb or 225 g)
- 1 stalk celery, chopped (1/4 lb or 115 g)
- 1 bunch fresh parsley (1 oz or 30 g)
- 1 bay leaf (1 leaf or 1 g)
- 1 medium zucchini, chopped (1/2 lb or 225 g)
- English Touch: a basil leaf
- American Touch: a pinch of garlic powder

## NUTRITIONAL VALUES:

- Calories: 30
- Carbohydrates: 7g
- Proteins: 1g
- Fats: 0g
- Fiber: 2g
- Sodium: 50mg
- Glucose: 3g
- Cholesterol: 0mg

## PROCEDURE:

1. In a large pot, bring the water to a boil.
2. Add the carrot, celery, parsley, bay leaf, and zucchini.
3. Reduce heat and simmer for 45 minutes.
4. Strain the broth, discarding the solids.
5. In a blender, combine the cooked zucchini from the broth with 1 cup of the clear broth and blend until smooth to create the zucchini cream.
6. Add the zucchini cream back into the pot with the clear broth.
7. For the English Touch, add a basil leaf as garnish.
8. For the American Touch, add a pinch of garlic powder to the soup.
9. Serve warm.

## SUGGESTED SUBSTITUTIONS:

- For parsley, you can use cilantro.
- For bay leaves, you can use thyme.

# Clear Vegetable Soup

| Preparation Time | Cooking Time | Total Time | Difficulty |
|---|---|---|---|
| 10 minutes | 45 minutes | 55 minutes | Easy |

**Servings**

1 person (For more people, multiply the ingredients by the number of people)

## INGREDIENTS:

- 4 cups water (32 fl oz or 950 ml)
- 1 medium carrot, peeled and chopped (1/2 lb or 225 g)
- 1 stalk celery, chopped (1/4 lb or 115 g)
- 1 bunch fresh parsley (1 oz or 30 g)
- 1 bay leaf (1 leaf or 1 g)
- 1 cup clear vegetable soup (vegetable broth without fat and solid pieces)
- English Touch: a bay leaf during cooking
- American Touch: a pinch of cayenne pepper

## PROCEDURE:

1. In a large pot, bring the water to a boil.
2. Add the carrot, celery, parsley, and bay leaf.
3. Reduce heat and simmer for 45 minutes.
4. Strain the broth, discarding the solids.
5. Add the clear vegetable broth to the strained broth.
6. For the English Touch, add a bay leaf during cooking.
7. For the American Touch, add a pinch of cayenne pepper.
8. Serve warm.

## NUTRITIONAL VALUES:

- Calories: 30
- Carbohydrates: 7g
- Proteins: 1g
- Fats: 0g
- Fiber: 2g
- Sodium: 50mg
- Glucose: 3g
- Cholesterol: 0mg

## SUGGESTED SUBSTITUTIONS:

- For parsley, you can use cilantro.
- For bay leaves, you can use thyme.

# Potato Cream Soup

| Preparation Time | Cooking Time | Total Time | Difficulty |
|---|---|---|---|
| 10 minutes | 45 minutes | 55 minutes | Easy |

**Servings**
1 person (For more people, multiply the ingredients by the number of people)

## INGREDIENTS:
- 4 cups water (32 fl oz or 950 ml)
- 1 medium carrot, peeled and chopped (1/2 lb or 225 g)
- 1 stalk celery, chopped (1/4 lb or 115 g)
- 1 bunch fresh parsley (1 oz or 30 g)
- 1 bay leaf (1 leaf or 1 g)
- 1 medium potato, peeled and chopped (1/2 lb or 225 g)
- English Touch: a bit of nutmeg
- American Touch: a pinch of chives

## PROCEDURE:
1. In a large pot, bring the water to a boil.
2. Add the carrot, celery, parsley, bay leaf, and potato.
3. Reduce heat and simmer for 45 minutes.
4. Strain the broth, discarding the solids.
5. In a blender, combine the cooked potato from the broth with 1 cup of the clear broth and blend until smooth to create the potato cream.
6. Add the potato cream back into the pot with the clear broth.
7. For the English Touch, add a bit of nutmeg.
8. For the American Touch, add a pinch of chives.
9. Serve warm.

## NUTRITIONAL VALUES:
- Calories: 30
- Carbohydrates: 7g
- Proteins: 1g
- Fats: 0g
- Fiber: 2g
- Sodium: 50mg
- Glucose: 3g
- Cholesterol: 0mg

## SUGGESTED SUBSTITUTIONS:
- For parsley, you can use cilantro.
- For bay leaves, you can use thyme.

# Clear Fish Soup

| Preparation Time | Cooking Time | Total Time | Difficulty |
|---|---|---|---|
| 10 minutes | 45 minutes | 55 minutes | Easy |

**Servings**

1 person (For more people, multiply the ingredients by the number of people)

## INGREDIENTS:

- 4 cups water (32 fl oz or 950 ml)
- 1 medium carrot, peeled and chopped (1/2 lb or 225 g)
- 1 stalk celery, chopped (1/4 lb or 115 g)
- 1 bunch fresh parsley (1 oz or 30 g)
- 1 bay leaf (1 leaf or 1 g)
- 1 cup clear fish broth (fat-free and without solid pieces)
- English Touch: a lemon slice during cooking
- American Touch: a pinch of dill

## PROCEDURE:

1. In a large pot, bring the water to a boil.
2. Add the carrot, celery, parsley, and bay leaf.
3. Reduce heat and simmer for 45 minutes.
4. Strain the broth, discarding the solids.
5. Add the clear fish broth to the strained vegetable broth.
6. For the English Touch, add a lemon slice during cooking.
7. For the American Touch, add a pinch of dill.
8. Serve warm.

## NUTRITIONAL VALUES:

- Calories: 30
- Carbohydrates: 7g
- Proteins: 1g
- Fats: 0g
- Fiber: 2g
- Sodium: 50mg
- Glucose: 3g
- Cholesterol: 0mg

## SUGGESTED SUBSTITUTIONS:

- For parsley, you can use cilantro.
- For bay leaves, you can use thyme.

# Clear Turkey Broth

| Preparation Time | Cooking Time | Total Time | Difficulty |
|---|---|---|---|
| 10 minutes | 45 minutes | 55 minutes | Easy |

**Servings**
1 person (For more people, multiply the ingredients by the number of people)

## INGREDIENTS:

- 4 cups water (32 fl oz or 950 ml)
- 1 medium carrot, peeled and chopped (1/2 lb or 225 g)
- 1 stalk celery, chopped (1/4 lb or 115 g)
- 1 bunch fresh parsley (1 oz or 30 g)
- 1 bay leaf (1 leaf or 1 g)
- 1 cup clear turkey broth (fat-free and without solid pieces)
- English Touch: a splash of lemon juice
- American Touch: a sage leaf during cooking

## PROCEDURE:

1. In a large pot, bring the water to a boil.
2. Add the carrot, celery, parsley, and bay leaf.
3. Reduce heat and simmer for 45 minutes.
4. Strain the broth, discarding the solids.
5. Add the clear turkey broth to the strained vegetable broth.
6. For the English Touch, add a splash of lemon juice.
7. For the American Touch, add a sage leaf during cooking.
8. Serve warm.

## NUTRITIONAL VALUES:

- Calories: 30
- Carbohydrates: 7g
- Proteins: 1g
- Fats: 0g
- Fiber: 2g
- Sodium: 50mg
- Glucose: 3g
- Cholesterol: 0mg

## SUGGESTED SUBSTITUTIONS:

- For parsley, you can use cilantro.
- For bay leaves, you can use thyme.

# Fennel Cream Soup

| Preparation Time | Cooking Time | Total Time | Difficulty |
|---|---|---|---|
| 10 minutes | 45 minutes | 55 minutes | Easy |

**Servings**
1 person (For more people, multiply the ingredients by the number of people)

## INGREDIENTS:

- 4 cups water (32 fl oz or 950 ml)
- 1 medium carrot, peeled and chopped (1/2 lb or 225 g)
- 1 stalk celery, chopped (1/4 lb or 115 g)
- 1 bunch fresh parsley (1 oz or 30 g)
- 1 bay leaf (1 leaf or 1 g)
- 1 cup fennel cream (cooked fennel blended with clear broth)
- English Touch: a dill leaf
- American Touch: a pinch of white pepper

## PROCEDURE:

1. In a large pot, bring the water to a boil.
2. Add the carrot, celery, parsley, and bay leaf.
3. Reduce heat and simmer for 45 minutes.
4. Strain the broth, discarding the solids.
5. Blend the cooked fennel with the clear broth until smooth to create fennel cream.
6. For the English Touch, add a dill leaf.
7. For the American Touch, add a pinch of white pepper.
8. Serve warm.

## NUTRITIONAL VALUES:

- Calories: 30
- Carbohydrates: 7g
- Proteins: 1g
- Fats: 0g
- Fiber: 2g
- Sodium: 50mg
- Glucose: 3g
- Cholesterol: 0mg

## SUGGESTED SUBSTITUTIONS:

- For parsley, you can use cilantro.
- For bay leaves, you can use thyme.

# Herbed Chicken Broth

| Preparation Time | Cooking Time | Total Time | Difficulty |
|---|---|---|---|
| 10 minutes | 20 minutes | 30 minutes | Easy |

**Servings**
1 person (For more people, multiply the ingredients by the number of people)

## INGREDIENTS:

- 1 cup clear chicken broth (fat-free and without solid pieces)
- 4 cups water (32 fl oz or 950 ml)
- 1 medium carrot, peeled and chopped (1/2 lb or 225 g)
- 1 stalk celery, chopped (1/4 lb or 115 g)
- 1 bunch fresh parsley (1 oz or 30 g)
- 1 bay leaf (1 leaf or 1 g)
- English Touch: a fresh thyme leaf
- American Touch: a pinch of black pepper

## PROCEDURE:

1. In a large pot, bring the water to a boil.
2. Add the chopped carrot, celery, parsley, and bay leaf.
3. Reduce heat and simmer for 20 minutes.
4. Strain the vegetable broth, discarding the solids.
5. Add the clear chicken broth to the strained vegetable broth.
6. For the English Touch, add a fresh thyme leaf.
7. For the American Touch, add a pinch of black pepper.
8. Heat the broth until it is warm, then serve.

## NUTRITIONAL VALUES: (PER SERVING)

- Calories: 30
- Carbohydrates: 7g
- Proteins: 1g
- Fats: 0g
- Fiber: 2g
- Sodium: 50mg
- Glucose: 3g
- Cholesterol: 0mg

## SUGGESTED SUBSTITUTIONS:

- For parsley, you can use cilantro.
- For bay leaves, you can use thyme.

# Pumpkin Cream Soup

| Preparation Time | Cooking Time | Total Time | Difficulty |
|---|---|---|---|
| 15 minutes | 30 minutes | 45 minutes | Easy |

**Servings**
2 people (For more servings, adjust quantities accordingly)

## INGREDIENTS:

- 2 cups clear vegetable broth (see Clear Vegetable Broth recipe for ingredients and procedure)
- 1 cup cooked pumpkin, blended into a creamy consistency
- 2 sage leaves (for English Touch) or a pinch of nutmeg (for American Touch)

## PROCEDURE:

1. In a medium pot, combine the clear vegetable broth and the blended pumpkin cream.
2. Bring to a gentle boil over medium heat.
3. Add the sage leaves (for English Touch) or nutmeg (for American Touch), and stir well.
4. Reduce heat to low and simmer for 30 minutes, stirring occasionally.
5. Serve hot, garnished with a sage leaf or a sprinkle of nutmeg if desired.

## NUTRITIONAL VALUES:

- Calories: 60
- Carbohydrates: 12g
- Proteins: 2g
- Fats: 0.5g
- Fiber: 4g
- Sodium: 80mg
- Glucose: 5g
- Cholesterol: 0mg

## SUGGESTED SUBSTITUTIONS:

- Instead of sage leaves, you can use rosemary for a different herbaceous flavor.
- For a richer texture, replace part of the clear vegetable broth with coconut milk.

# Light Vegetable Soup

| Preparation Time | Cooking Time | Total Time | Difficulty |
|---|---|---|---|
| 10 minutes | 30 minutes | 40 minutes | Easy |

**Servings**
1 person (For more people, multiply the ingredients by the number of people)

## INGREDIENTS:

- 1 cup light vegetable soup (vegetable broth without fat and solid pieces)
- 4 cups water (32 fl oz or 950 ml)
- 1 medium carrot, peeled and chopped (1/2 lb or 225 g)
- 1 stalk celery, chopped (1/4 lb or 115 g)
- 1 bunch fresh parsley (1 oz or 30 g)
- 1 bay leaf (1 leaf or 1 g)
- English Touch: a bay leaf during cooking
- American Touch: a pinch of cayenne pepper

## NUTRITIONAL VALUES: (PER SERVING)

- Calories: 30
- Carbohydrates: 7g
- Proteins: 1g
- Fats: 0g
- Fiber: 2g
- Sodium: 50mg
- Glucose: 3g
- Cholesterol: 0mg

## SUGGESTED SUBSTITUTIONS:

- For parsley, you can use cilantro.
- For bay leaves, you can use thyme.

## PROCEDURE:

1. In a large pot, bring the water to a boil.
2. Add the chopped carrot, celery, parsley, and bay leaf.
3. Reduce heat and simmer for 30 minutes.
4. Strain the vegetable broth, discarding the solids.
5. For the English Touch, add a bay leaf during cooking.
6. For the American Touch, add a pinch of cayenne pepper.
7. Heat the broth until it is warm, then serve.

# Herbed Beef Broth

| Preparation Time | Cooking Time | Total Time | Difficulty |
|---|---|---|---|
| 5 minutes | 30 minutes | 35 minutes | Easy |

**Servings**
1 person (For more people, multiply the ingredients by the number of people)

## INGREDIENTS:

- 1 cup clear beef broth (fat-free and without solid pieces)
- English Touch: Add a rosemary leaf
- American Touch: Add a pinch of black pepper

## NUTRITIONAL VALUES:

- Calories: 15
- Carbohydrates: 0g
- Proteins: 3g
- Fats: 0g
- Fiber: 0g
- Sodium: 200mg
- Glucose: 0g
- Cholesterol: 0mg

## PROCEDURE:

1. In a small pot, bring the clear beef broth to a gentle simmer over medium heat.
2. Add the rosemary leaf to the broth.
3. Continue to simmer for 30 minutes, allowing the flavors to infuse.
4. Remove the rosemary leaf and discard.
5. Add a pinch of black pepper for an American touch.
6. Serve warm.

## SUGGESTED SUBSTITUTIONS:

- For rosemary, you can use thyme.
- For black pepper, you can use white pepper.

# Soup Celery Cream

| Preparation Time | Cooking Time | Total Time | Difficulty |
|---|---|---|---|
| 10 minutes | 35 minutes | 45 minutes | Easy |

**Servings**
1 person (For more people, multiply the ingredients by the number of people)

## INGREDIENTS:

- 2 cups water (480 ml)
- 2 stalks celery, chopped (115 g)
- 1/2 medium potato, peeled and chopped (75 g)
- 1/2 small onion, chopped (50 g)
- 1/2 cup clear vegetable broth (120 ml)
- English Touch: 1 parsley leaf (1 g)
- American Touch: A pinch of garlic powder (1 g)

## PROCEDURE:

1. In a medium saucepan, bring the water to a boil.
2. Add the chopped celery, potato, and onion to the pot. Reduce heat to medium-low and simmer for 25 minutes, until the vegetables are tender.
3. Remove from heat and let it cool slightly.
4. Transfer the cooked vegetables and cooking liquid to a blender. Add the clear vegetable broth and blend until smooth.
5. Return the blended mixture to the saucepan and heat over low heat until warmed through.
6. For an English touch, add the parsley leaf before serving.
7. For an American touch, stir in a pinch of garlic powder before serving.
8. Serve warm.

## NUTRITIONAL VALUES:

- Calories: 70
- Carbohydrates: 15g
- Proteins: 2g
- Fats: 0g
- Fiber: 2g
- Sodium: 60mg
- Glucose: 3g
- Cholesterol: 0mg

## SUGGESTED SUBSTITUTIONS:

- For celery, you can use fennel.
- For potatoes, you can use cauliflower.
- For clear vegetable broth, you can use clear chicken broth

## Breakfast

# Rice Porridge

| Preparation Time | Cooking Time | Total Time | Difficulty |
|:---:|:---:|:---:|:---:|
| **5 minutes** | **25 minutes** | **30 minutes** | Easy |

**Servings**
1 person (For more servings, multiply the ingredients by the number of people)

### INGREDIENTS:
- 1/4 cup rice (50 g)
- 2 cups water (480 ml)
- 1/2 cup almond milk (120 ml)
- 1 tbsp maple syrup (American touch) (15 ml)
- 1 tbsp blackcurrant jam (British touch) (20 g)

### PROCEDURE:
1. Rinse the rice under cold water until the water runs clear.
2. In a medium pot, bring the water to a boil over medium-high heat.
3. Add the rice to the boiling water, reduce the heat to low, and cover the pot.
4. Simmer the rice for 20 minutes, stirring occasionally, until the rice is soft and has absorbed most of the water.
5. Add the almond milk and continue to cook for another 5 minutes, stirring frequently until the mixture is creamy and smooth.
6. Remove from heat and serve hot.
7. For the American touch, drizzle maple syrup over the porridge.
8. For the British touch, top the porridge with blackcurrant jam.

### NUTRITIONAL VALUES:
- **Calories:** 220
- **Carbohydrates:** 45g
- **Proteins:** 3g
- **Fats:** 3g
- **Fiber:** 1g
- **Sodium:** 60mg
- **Glucose:** 12g
- **Cholesterol:** 0mg

### SUGGESTED SUBSTITUTIONS:
- Instead of almond milk, you can use rice milk or oat milk.
- Instead of maple syrup, you can use honey (if not vegan) or agave syrup.

This rice porridge recipe is designed to be gentle on the digestive system while offering comforting and flavorful touches depending on your preference for a British or American flair.

# Banana and Yogurt Smoothie

| Preparation Time | Cooking Time | Total Time | Difficulty |
|:---:|:---:|:---:|:---:|
| 5 minutes | 0 minutes | 5 minutes | Easy |

**Servings**
1 person (For more servings, multiply the ingredients by the number of people)

## INGREDIENTS:
- 1 ripe banana, peeled and sliced
- 1/2 cup natural yogurt (120 ml)
- 1 extra banana (for American touch), sliced
- 1 tbsp eucalyptus honey (for British touch) (15 ml)

## PROCEDURE:
1. Place the sliced ripe banana and natural yogurt in a blender.
2. Blend until smooth and creamy, about 30 seconds to 1 minute.
3. Pour into a serving glass.
4. For the American touch, garnish with slices of the extra banana.
5. For the British touch, drizzle eucalyptus honey over the top.

This Banana and Yogurt Smoothie is a refreshing and nutritious option, adaptable with either an American or British touch depending on your preference for additional banana slices or a drizzle of honey.

## NUTRITIONAL VALUES:
- **Calories:** 250
- **Carbohydrates:** 54g
- **Proteins:** 8g
- **Fats:** 2g
- **Fiber:** 5g
- **Sodium:** 90mg
- **Glucose:** 40g
- **Cholesterol:** 5mg

## SUGGESTED SUBSTITUTIONS:
- Instead of natural yogurt, you can use Greek yogurt for a thicker consistency.
- Instead of eucalyptus honey, you can use regular honey or agave syrup for sweetness.

# Oatmeal Cream

| Preparation Time | Cooking Time | Total Time | Difficulty |
|:---:|:---:|:---:|:---:|
| 5 minutes | 10 minutes | 15 minutes | Easy |

**Servings**
1 person (For more servings, multiply the ingredients by the number of people)

## INGREDIENTS:
- 1/4 cup oats (20 g)
- 1 cup water (240 ml)
- 1 tbsp honey (American touch) (15 ml)
- 2 tbsp apple compote (British touch) (30 g)

## PROCEDURE:
1. In a small pot, combine the oats and water.
2. Bring the mixture to a boil over medium-high heat.
3. Reduce the heat to low and simmer for 10 minutes, stirring occasionally until the oats are soft and the mixture is creamy.
4. Remove from heat and let cool slightly.
5. For the American touch, stir in the honey.
6. For the British touch, top with apple compote.

This Oatmeal Cream recipe offers a comforting and gentle option for those looking to minimize intestinal irritation. The dish can be easily customized with either a touch of honey for sweetness or apple compote for a fruity flavor.

## NUTRITIONAL VALUES:
- **Calories:** 150
- **Carbohydrates:** 30g
- **Proteins:** 3g
- **Fats:** 2g
- **Fiber:** 2g
- **Sodium:** 0mg
- **Glucose:** 12g
- **Cholesterol:** 0mg

## SUGGESTED SUBSTITUTIONS:
- Instead of honey, you can use maple syrup or agave syrup for sweetness.
- Instead of apple compote, you can use pear compote or mashed bananas.
- Avoid adding any whole grains, unpeeled fruits, or raw vegetables to prevent aggravating symptoms of diverticulitis.

# Potato Pancakes

| Preparation Time | Cooking Time | Total Time | Difficulty |
|---|---|---|---|
| 10 minutes | 15 minutes | 25 minutes | Easy |

**Servings**
1 person (For more people, multiply the ingredients by the number of people)

## INGREDIENTS:

- 1 medium potato, peeled and grated (150 g)
- 1/4 cup milk (60 ml)
- 1 egg, beaten
- 1 tbsp maple syrup (American touch) (15 ml)
- 2 tbsp applesauce (British touch) (30 g)
- 1/4 tsp salt (1 g)
- 1 tbsp vegetable oil (15 ml)

## PROCEDURE:

1. In a bowl, combine the grated potato, milk, beaten egg, and salt. Mix well.
2. Heat the vegetable oil in a non-stick frying pan over medium heat.
3. Drop spoonfuls of the potato mixture into the pan, flattening them into pancake shapes.
4. Cook for about 3-4 minutes on each side, or until golden brown and crispy.
5. Remove the pancakes from the pan and drain on paper towels.
6. For the American touch, drizzle the pancakes with maple syrup.
7. For the British touch, serve the pancakes with a side of applesauce.

## NUTRITIONAL VALUES:

- **Calories:** 250
- **Carbohydrates:** 30g
- **Proteins:** 6g
- **Fats:** 12g
- **Fiber:** 2g
- **Sodium:** 300mg
- **Glucose:** 8g
- **Cholesterol:** 100mg

## SUGGESTED SUBSTITUTIONS:

- Instead of milk, you can use almond milk or rice milk.
- Instead of vegetable oil, you can use olive oil or avocado oil.

These Potato Pancakes provide a savory base that can be enjoyed with either the sweetness of maple syrup or the fruity flavor of applesauce, making them a versatile and gentle option for those managing diverticulitis.

# Soft Scrambled Eggs on Toast

| Preparation Time | Cooking Time | Total Time | Difficulty |
|---|---|---|---|
| 5 minutes | 5 minutes | 10 minutes | Easy |

**Servings**
1 person (For more people, multiply the ingredients by the number of people)

## INGREDIENTS:

- 2 large eggs
- 1 tbsp olive oil (15 ml)
- 2 slices white bread
- Salt to taste (optional)
- 1 extra egg (American touch)
- 1 extra slice of white toast (British touch)

## PROCEDURE:

1. In a bowl, beat the eggs until well mixed.
2. Heat the olive oil in a non-stick frying pan over low heat.
3. Pour the beaten eggs into the pan and let them sit undisturbed for a few seconds.
4. Using a spatula, gently stir the eggs, pushing them from the edges towards the center, until they are softly scrambled and just set, about 3-5 minutes.
5. While the eggs are cooking, toast the slices of white bread.
6. Place the toast on a plate and top with the soft scrambled eggs.
7. For the American touch, scramble an additional egg and add it to the plate.
8. For the British touch, serve an extra slice of white toast on the side.

## NUTRITIONAL VALUES:

- **Calories:** 250
- **Carbohydrates:** 20g
- **Proteins:** 12g
- **Fats:** 15g
- **Fiber:** 1g
- **Sodium:** 300mg
- **Glucose:** 2g
- **Cholesterol:** 370mg

## SUGGESTED SUBSTITUTIONS:

- Instead of olive oil, you can use butter or avocado oil.
- Instead of white bread, you can use gluten-free bread if needed.

This Soft Scrambled Eggs on Toast recipe is a gentle, easy-to-digest meal that can be customized with an extra egg for a hearty American touch or an extra slice of white toast for a traditional British touch.

# Tapioca Pudding

| Preparation Time | Cooking Time | Total Time | Difficulty |
|---|---|---|---|
| 10 minutes | 15 minutes | 25 minutes | Easy |

**Servings**
1 person (For more people, multiply the ingredients by the number of people)

## INGREDIENTS:
- 1/4 cup tapioca pearls (50 g)
- 1 cup rice milk (240 ml)
- 1 tbsp whipped cream (American touch) (15 ml)
- 1/2 tsp vanilla extract (British touch) (2.5 ml)

## PROCEDURE:
1. In a medium saucepan, soak the tapioca pearls in rice milk for 5 minutes.
2. Place the saucepan over medium heat and bring the mixture to a gentle boil, stirring frequently.
3. Reduce the heat to low and simmer for 10 minutes, stirring continuously, until the tapioca pearls are transparent and the mixture has thickened.
4. Remove from heat and let the pudding cool slightly.
5. For the American touch, top with a dollop of whipped cream before serving.
6. For the British touch, stir in the vanilla extract before serving.

## NUTRITIONAL VALUES:
- **Calories:** 180
- **Carbohydrates:** 35g
- **Proteins:** 2g
- **Fats:** 4g
- **Fiber:** 1g
- **Sodium:** 50mg
- **Glucose:** 12g
- **Cholesterol:** 0mg

## SUGGESTED SUBSTITUTIONS:
- Instead of rice milk, you can use almond milk or coconut milk.
- Instead of whipped cream, you can use coconut whipped cream or omit it altogether for a lighter version.

This Tapioca Pudding recipe offers a smooth and creamy dessert option, with the choice of adding whipped cream for an American touch or vanilla extract for a British touch, making it suitable for a gentle, easy-to-digest treat.

# Blueberry Jelly

| Preparation Time | Cooking Time | Total Time | Difficulty |
|---|---|---|---|
| 5 minutes | 5 minutes | 2 hours 10 minutes (including chilling time) | Easy |

**Servings**
1 person (For more people, multiply the ingredients by the number of people)

## INGREDIENTS:

- 1 tbsp gelatin powder (10 g)
- 1 cup blueberry juice (240 ml)
- 1 tbsp whipped cream (American touch) (15 ml)
- 1 tbsp extra blueberries (British touch) (15 g)

## PROCEDURE:

1. In a small bowl, sprinkle the gelatin over 1/4 cup (60 ml) of the blueberry juice. Let it sit for 5 minutes to soften.
2. In a small saucepan, heat the remaining 3/4 cup (180 ml) of blueberry juice over medium heat until warm but not boiling.
3. Add the softened gelatin mixture to the warm juice and stir until the gelatin is completely dissolved.
4. Pour the mixture into a mold or serving dish.
5. Chill in the refrigerator for at least 2 hours or until set.
6. For the American touch, top the set jelly with a dollop of whipped cream before serving.
7. For the British touch, garnish the set jelly with extra blueberries before serving.

## NUTRITIONAL VALUES:

- **Calories:** 100
- **Carbohydrates:** 22g
- **Proteins:** 2g
- **Fats:** 1g
- **Fiber:** 1g
- **Sodium:** 10mg
- **Glucose:** 20g
- **Cholesterol:** 0mg

## SUGGESTED SUBSTITUTIONS:

- Instead of blueberry juice, you can use another fruit juice like apple or grape juice.
- Instead of whipped cream, you can use a non-dairy whipped topping.

This Blueberry Jelly recipe is a light, refreshing, and easy-to-digest dessert that can be enhanced with whipped cream for an American touch or extra blueberries for a British touch.

# Natural Apple Jelly

| Preparation Time | Cooking Time | Total Time | Difficulty |
|---|---|---|---|
| 5 minutes | 5 minutes | 2 hours 10 minutes (including chilling time) | Easy |

**Servings**
1 person (For more people, multiply the ingredients by the number of people)

## INGREDIENTS:
- 1 tbsp gelatin powder (10 g)
- 1 cup apple juice (240 ml)
- 1 tbsp whipped cream (American touch) (15 ml)
- 1 tbsp finely chopped peeled apple (British touch) (15 g)

## PROCEDURE:
1. In a small bowl, sprinkle the gelatin over 1/4 cup (60 ml) of the apple juice. Let it sit for 5 minutes to soften.
2. In a small saucepan, heat the remaining 3/4 cup (180 ml) of apple juice over medium heat until warm but not boiling.
3. Add the softened gelatin mixture to the warm juice and stir until the gelatin is completely dissolved.
4. Pour the mixture into a mold or serving dish.
5. Chill in the refrigerator for at least 2 hours or until set.
6. For the American touch, top the set jelly with a dollop of whipped cream before serving.
7. For the British touch, garnish the set jelly with finely chopped peeled apple before serving.

## NUTRITIONAL VALUES:
- **Calories:** 90
- **Carbohydrates:** 20g
- **Proteins:** 2g
- **Fats:** 1g
- **Fiber:** 0g
- **Sodium:** 5mg
- **Glucose:** 19g
- **Cholesterol:** 0mg

## SUGGESTED SUBSTITUTIONS:
- Instead of apple juice, you can use another clear juice like pear or white grape juice.
- Instead of whipped cream, you can use a non-dairy whipped topping.

This Natural Apple Jelly recipe is a simple, light, and refreshing dessert, perfect for a low-residue diet. It can be enhanced with whipped cream for an American touch or finely chopped peeled apple for a British touch

# Applesauce

| Preparation Time | Cooking Time | Total Time | Difficulty |
|---|---|---|---|
| 10 minutes | 20 minutes | 30 minutes | Easy |

**Servings**
1 person (For more people, multiply the ingredients by the number of people)

## INGREDIENTS: •
- 2 large apples, peeled, cored, and chopped (about 350 g)
- 1/4 cup water (60 ml)
- 1/2 tsp cinnamon (American touch) (1 g)
- 1 extra apple, peeled, cored, and finely chopped (British touch) (175 g)

## PROCEDURE:
1. In a medium saucepan, combine the chopped apples and water.
2. Bring the mixture to a boil over medium heat.
3. Reduce the heat to low, cover, and simmer for about 15-20 minutes, or until the apples are soft and tender.
4. Remove from heat and let it cool slightly.
5. Mash the apples with a fork or potato masher until you reach the desired consistency.
6. For the American touch, stir in the cinnamon before serving.
7. For the British touch, top with finely chopped extra apple before serving.

## NUTRITIONAL VALUES:
- **Calories:** 120
- **Carbohydrates:** 30g
- **Proteins:** 0g
- **Fats:** 0g
- **Fiber:** 3g
- **Sodium:** 0mg
- **Glucose:** 25g
- **Cholesterol:** 0mg

## SUGGESTED SUBSTITUTIONS:
- Instead of water, you can use apple juice for added flavor.
- Instead of cinnamon, you can use a small amount of nutmeg or omit it altogether.

This Applesauce recipe provides a smooth, easy-to-digest dish suitable for a low-residue diet. It can be enhanced with cinnamon for an American touch or topped with extra finely chopped apple for a British touch.

# Vegetable Broth

| Preparation Time | Cooking Time | Total Time | Difficulty |
|---|---|---|---|
| 10 minutes | 30 minutes | 40 minutes | Easy |

**Servings**
1 person (For more people, multiply the ingredients by the number of people)

## INGREDIENTS:
- 4 cups vegetable broth (950 ml)
- 1 cup mixed vegetables, finely chopped (120 g)
- 1/4 cup sweet corn (American touch) (40 g)
- 2 tbsp pearl barley (British touch) (30 g)

## PROCEDURE:
1. In a large pot, bring the vegetable broth to a boil over medium heat.
2. Add the mixed vegetables and reduce the heat to low.
3. Simmer for 20 minutes until the vegetables are tender.
4. For the American touch, add sweet corn and cook for an additional 5 minutes.
5. For the British touch, add pearl barley and cook for an additional 10 minutes, until the barley is tender.
6. Serve warm.

## NUTRITIONAL VALUES:
- **Calories:** 80
- **Carbohydrates:** 15g
- **Proteins:** 2g
- **Fats:** 0g
- **Fiber:** 3g
- **Sodium:** 300mg
- **Glucose:** 5g
- **Cholesterol:** 0mg

## SUGGESTED SUBSTITUTIONS:
- Instead of vegetable broth, you can use chicken or beef broth if not vegetarian.

# Rice Pudding

| Preparation Time | Cooking Time | Total Time | Difficulty |
|---|---|---|---|
| 5 minutes | 25 minutes | 30 minutes | Easy |

**Servings**
1 person (For more people, multiply the ingredients by the number of people)

## INGREDIENTS:
- 1/4 cup rice (50 g)
- 1 cup almond milk (240 ml)
- 1 tbsp dried blueberries (American touch) (15 g)
- 1 tbsp Demerara sugar (British touch) (15 g)

## PROCEDURE:
1. In a medium saucepan, combine the rice and almond milk.
2. Bring to a boil over medium heat, then reduce the heat to low and simmer for 20-25 minutes, stirring occasionally, until the rice is tender and the mixture is creamy.
3. For the American touch, stir in dried blueberries before serving.
4. For the British touch, sprinkle Demerara sugar on top before serving.

## NUTRITIONAL VALUES:
- **Calories:** 200
- **Carbohydrates:** 40g
- **Proteins:** 3g
- **Fats:** 2g
- **Fiber:** 1g
- **Sodium:** 50mg
- **Glucose:** 20g
- **Cholesterol:** 0mg

## SUGGESTED SUBSTITUTIONS:
- Instead of almond milk, you can use regular milk or other non-dairy milk.

# Natural Yogurt

| Preparation Time | Cooking Time | Total Time | Difficulty |
|---|---|---|---|
| 2 minutes | 0 minutes | 2 minutes | Easy |

**Servings**
1 person (For more people, multiply the ingredients by the number of people)

## INGREDIENTS:
- 1 cup natural yogurt (240 g)
- 1 tbsp acacia honey (American touch) (15 ml)
- 1 tbsp sugar-free fruit compote (British touch) (15 g)

## PROCEDURE:
1. Serve the natural yogurt in a bowl.
2. For the American touch, drizzle acacia honey over the yogurt.
3. For the British touch, top with sugar-free fruit compote.

## NUTRITIONAL VALUES:
- **Calories:** 150
- **Carbohydrates:** 20g
- **Proteins:** 8g
- **Fats:** 5g
- **Fiber:** 0g
- **Sodium:** 80mg
- **Glucose:** 18g
- **Cholesterol:** 10mg

## SUGGESTED SUBSTITUTIONS:
- Instead of acacia honey, you can use maple syrup or agave nectar.

# Mashed Bananas

| Preparation Time | Cooking Time | Total Time | Difficulty |
|---|---|---|---|
| 3 minutes | 0 minutes | 3 minutes | Easy |

**Servings**
1 person (For more people, multiply the ingredients by the number of people)

## INGREDIENTS:

- 1 large ripe banana (120 g)
- 1 tbsp peanut butter (American touch) (15 g)
- 1 tbsp golden syrup (British touch) (15 ml)

## PROCEDURE:

1. Peel and mash the banana in a bowl until smooth.
2. For the American touch, mix in peanut butter.
3. For the British touch, drizzle golden syrup over the mashed banana before serving.

## NUTRITIONAL VALUES:

- **Calories:** 150
- **Carbohydrates:** 30g
- **Proteins:** 2g
- **Fats:** 3g
- **Fiber:** 3g
- **Sodium:** 2mg
- **Glucose:** 20g
- **Cholesterol:** 0mg

## SUGGESTED SUBSTITUTIONS:

- Instead of peanut butter, you can use almond butter or sunflower seed butter.

# Pear and Apple Smoothie

| Preparation Time | Cooking Time | Total Time | Difficulty |
|---|---|---|---|
| 5 minutes | 0 minutes | 5 minutes | Easy |

**Servings**
1 person (For more people, multiply the ingredients by the number of people)

## INGREDIENTS:

- 1 ripe pear, peeled and chopped (150 g)
- 1 ripe apple, peeled and chopped (150 g)
- 1/4 tsp vanilla extract (American touch) (1 ml)
- 1/4 tsp ground cinnamon (British touch) (1 g)

## PROCEDURE:

1. In a blender, combine the chopped pear and apple.
2. Blend until smooth.
3. For the American touch, add vanilla extract and blend again.
4. For the British touch, sprinkle ground cinnamon on top before serving.

## NUTRITIONAL VALUES:

- **Calories:** 120
- **Carbohydrates:** 30g
- **Proteins:** 1g
- **Fats:** 0g
- **Fiber:** 5g
- **Sodium:** 2mg
- **Glucose:** 25g
- **Cholesterol:** 0mg

## SUGGESTED SUBSTITUTIONS:

- Instead of using fresh fruits, you can use canned or jarred fruits in natural juice.

# Clear Broths and Soups

## Clear Vegetable Broth

| Preparation Time | Cooking Time | Total Time | Difficulty |
|---|---|---|---|
| 10 minutes | 45 minutes | 55 minutes | Easy |

**Servings**
1 person (For more people, multiply the ingredients by the number of people)

### INGREDIENTS:
- 4 cups water (950 ml)
- 1 medium carrot, peeled and chopped (225 g)
- 1 stalk celery, chopped (115 g)
- 1 bunch fresh parsley (American touch) (30 g)
- 1 bay leaf (British touch) (1 leaf or 1 g)

### PROCEDURE:
1. In a large pot, bring the water to a boil.
2. Add the carrot, celery, and bay leaf.
3. Reduce heat and simmer for 45 minutes.
4. For the American touch, add fresh parsley in the last 10 minutes of cooking.
5. Strain the broth, discarding the solids.
6. Serve warm.

### NUTRITIONAL VALUES:
- **Calories:** 30
- **Carbohydrates:** 7g
- **Proteins:** 1g
- **Fats:** 0g
- **Fiber:** 2g
- **Sodium:** 50mg
- **Glucose:** 3g
- **Cholesterol:** 0mg

### SUGGESTED SUBSTITUTIONS:
- Instead of fresh parsley, use cilantro.
- Instead of bay leaf, use thyme.

## Light Chicken Soup

| Preparation Time | Cooking Time | Total Time | Difficulty |
|---|---|---|---|
| 15 minutes | 45 minutes | 60 minutes | Easy |

**Servings**
1 person (For more people, multiply the ingredients by the number of people)

### INGREDIENTS:
- 4 cups water (950 ml)
- 1/2 cup cooked chicken, shredded (100 g)
- 1 medium carrot, peeled and chopped (225 g)
- 1 tsp thyme (American touch) (2 g)
- 1 sprig rosemary (British touch) (1 g)

### PROCEDURE:
1. In a large pot, bring the water to a boil.
2. Add the chicken, carrot, and rosemary.
3. Reduce heat and simmer for 45 minutes.
4. For the American touch, add thyme in the last 10 minutes of cooking.
5. Strain the broth, discarding the solids.
6. Serve warm.

### NUTRITIONAL VALUES:
- **Calories:** 150
- **Carbohydrates:** 10g
- **Proteins:** 20g
- **Fats:** 3g
- **Fiber:** 2g
- **Sodium:** 60mg
- **Glucose:** 2g
- **Cholesterol:** 45mg

### SUGGESTED SUBSTITUTIONS:
- Instead of thyme, use oregano.
- Instead of rosemary, use sage.

# Delicate Beef Broth

| Preparation Time | Cooking Time | Total Time | Difficulty |
|---|---|---|---|
| 10 minutes | 60 minutes | 70 minutes | Easy |

**Servings**
1 person (For more people, multiply the ingredients by the number of people)

## INGREDIENTS:
- 4 cups water (950 ml)
- 1/2 lb lean beef, cubed (225 g)
- 1 small onion, chopped (70 g)
- 1/2 tsp garlic powder (American touch) (1 g)
- 2 cloves (British touch) (2 g)

## PROCEDURE:
1. In a large pot, bring the water to a boil.
2. Add the beef, onion, and cloves.
3. Reduce heat and simmer for 60 minutes.
4. For the American touch, add garlic powder in the last 10 minutes of cooking.
5. Strain the broth, discarding the solids.
6. Serve warm.

## NUTRITIONAL VALUES:
- **Calories:** 200
- **Carbohydrates:** 5g
- **Proteins:** 25g
- **Fats:** 10g
- **Fiber:** 1g
- **Sodium:** 70mg
- **Glucose:** 1g
- **Cholesterol:** 60mg

## SUGGESTED SUBSTITUTIONS:
- Instead of garlic powder, use onion powder.
- Instead of cloves, use allspice.

# Potato and Leek Soup

| Preparation Time | Cooking Time | Total Time | Difficulty |
|---|---|---|---|
| 15 minutes | 40 minutes | 55 minutes | Easy |

**Servings**
1 person (For more people, multiply the ingredients by the number of people)

## INGREDIENTS:
- 4 cups vegetable broth (950 ml)
- 1 medium potato, peeled and chopped (200 g)
- 1 leek, white part only, chopped (150 g)
- 1 tsp dill (American touch) (1 g)
- 1 tbsp chopped parsley (British touch) (4 g)

## PROCEDURE:
1. In a large pot, bring the vegetable broth to a boil.
2. Add the potato and leek.
3. Reduce heat and simmer for 30 minutes until vegetables are tender.
4. For the American touch, add dill in the last 10 minutes of cooking.
5. For the British touch, sprinkle chopped parsley before serving.
6. Blend until smooth if a creamier texture is desired.
7. Serve warm.

## NUTRITIONAL VALUES:
- **Calories:** 150
- **Carbohydrates:** 30g
- **Proteins:** 3g
- **Fats:** 1g
- **Fiber:** 3g
- **Sodium:** 400mg
- **Glucose:** 5g
- **Cholesterol:** 0mg

## SUGGESTED SUBSTITUTIONS:
- Instead of dill, use chives.
- Instead of parsley, use tarragon.

# Clear Turkey Consommé

| Preparation Time | Cooking Time | Total Time | Difficulty |
|---|---|---|---|
| 15 minutes | 60 minutes | 75 minutes | Easy |

**Servings**
1 person (For more people, multiply the ingredients by the number of people)

## INGREDIENTS:

- 4 cups water (950 ml)
- 1/2 lb turkey meat, cubed (225 g)
- 1 small onion, chopped (70 g)
- 1 sage leaf (American touch) (1 g)
- 1/2 tsp fennel seeds (British touch) (1 g)

## PROCEDURE:

1. In a large pot, bring the water to a boil.
2. Add the turkey, onion, and fennel seeds.
3. Reduce heat and simmer for 60 minutes.
4. For the American touch, add sage leaf in the last 10 minutes of cooking.
5. Strain the broth, discarding the solids.
6. Serve warm.

## NUTRITIONAL VALUES:

- **Calories:** 180
- **Carbohydrates:** 5g
- **Proteins:** 25g
- **Fats:** 5g
- **Fiber:** 1g
- **Sodium:** 60mg
- **Glucose:** 2g
- **Cholesterol:** 50mg

## SUGGESTED SUBSTITUTIONS:

- Instead of sage, use thyme.
- Instead of fennel seeds, use caraway seeds.

# Light Beet Soup

| Preparation Time | Cooking Time | Total Time | Difficulty |
|---|---|---|---|
| 10 minutes | 40 minutes | 50 minutes | Easy |

**Servings**
1 person (For more people, multiply the ingredients by the number of people)

## INGREDIENTS:

- 1 medium beet, peeled and chopped (150 g)
- 4 cups vegetable broth (950 ml)
- 1 tbsp lemon juice (15 ml)
- 1 tbsp sour cream (American touch) (15 g)
- 1/2 tsp ground cumin (British touch) (1 g)

## PROCEDURE:

1. In a large pot, bring the vegetable broth to a boil.
2. Add the chopped beet and reduce the heat to simmer.
3. Cook for 30 minutes, or until the beet is tender.
4. For the American touch, stir in sour cream.
5. For the British touch, add ground cumin.
6. Add lemon juice and stir well.
7. Serve warm.

## NUTRITIONAL VALUES:

- **Calories:** 70
- **Carbohydrates:** 15g
- **Proteins:** 2g
- **Fats:** 1g
- **Fiber:** 3g
- **Sodium:** 400mg
- **Glucose:** 10g
- **Cholesterol:** 2mg

## SUGGESTED SUBSTITUTIONS:

- Instead of sour cream, use Greek yogurt.
- Instead of ground cumin, use coriander.

# Light Fish Broth

| Preparation Time | Cooking Time | Total Time | Difficulty |
|---|---|---|---|
| 10 minutes | 30 minutes | 40 minutes | Easy |

**Servings**
1 person (For more people, multiply the ingredients by the number of people)

## INGREDIENTS:

- 1/2 lb lean fish filets (225 g)
- 4 cups water (950 ml)
- 1 stalk celery, chopped (115 g)
- 1 tbsp fresh cilantro (American touch) (4 g)
- 1 tsp lemon extract (British touch) (5 ml)

## PROCEDURE:

1. In a large pot, bring the water to a boil.
2. Add the fish filets and celery.
3. Reduce heat and simmer for 25 minutes.
4. For the American touch, add fresh cilantro in the last 5 minutes of cooking.
5. For the British touch, stir in lemon extract.
6. Strain the broth, discarding the solids.
7. Serve warm.

## NUTRITIONAL VALUES:

- **Calories:** 120
- **Carbohydrates:** 3g
- **Proteins:** 20g
- **Fats:** 2g
- **Fiber:** 1g
- **Sodium:** 100mg
- **Glucose:** 1g
- **Cholesterol:** 45mg

## SUGGESTED SUBSTITUTIONS:

- Instead of fresh cilantro, use parsley.
- Instead of lemon extract, use lime juice.

# Pumpkin and Carrot Soup

| Preparation Time | Cooking Time | Total Time | Difficulty |
|---|---|---|---|
| 15 minutes | 30 minutes | 45 minutes | Easy |

**Servings**
1 person (For more people, multiply the ingredients by the number of people)

## INGREDIENTS:

- 1 cup pumpkin, peeled and chopped (225 g)
- 1 medium carrot, peeled and chopped (75 g)
- 4 cups vegetable broth (950 ml)
- 1/2 tsp ground cinnamon (American touch) (1 g)
- 1 tsp fresh ginger, grated (British touch) (2 g)

## PROCEDURE:

1. In a large pot, bring the vegetable broth to a boil.
2. Add the pumpkin and carrot.
3. Reduce heat and simmer for 25 minutes, or until vegetables are tender.
4. For the American touch, add ground cinnamon.
5. For the British touch, stir in fresh ginger.
6. Blend the soup until smooth.
7. Serve warm.

## NUTRITIONAL VALUES:

- **Calories:** 80
- **Carbohydrates:** 18g
- **Proteins:** 2g
- **Fats:** 0g
- **Fiber:** 4g
- **Sodium:** 400mg
- **Glucose:** 8g
- **Cholesterol:** 0mg

## SUGGESTED SUBSTITUTIONS:

- Instead of ground cinnamon, use nutmeg.
- Instead of fresh ginger, use dried ginger.

# Apple and Banana Smoothie

| Preparation Time | Cooking Time | Total Time | Difficulty |
|---|---|---|---|
| 5 minutes | 0 minutes | 5 minutes | Easy |

**Servings**
1 person (For more people, multiply the ingredients by the number of people)

## INGREDIENTS:

- 1 apple, peeled, cored, and chopped (150 g)
- 1 ripe banana (120 g)
- 1 cup coconut water (240 ml)
- 2 tbsp Greek yogurt (American touch) (30 g)
- 1 tbsp lavender honey (British touch) (15 ml)

## PROCEDURE:

1. Place the chopped apple, banana, coconut water, Greek yogurt, and lavender honey in a blender.
2. Blend until smooth.
3. Serve immediately.

## NUTRITIONAL VALUES:

- **Calories:** 220
- **Carbohydrates:** 52g
- **Proteins:** 4g
- **Fats:** 1g
- **Fiber:** 6g
- **Sodium:** 180mg
- **Glucose:** 30g
- **Cholesterol:** 0mg

## SUGGESTED SUBSTITUTIONS:

- Substitute Greek yogurt with coconut milk for a dairy-free option.
- Replace lavender honey with maple syrup for a different sweetness.

# Carrot and Ginger Smoothie

| Preparation Time | Cooking Time | Total Time | Difficulty |
|---|---|---|---|
| 5 minutes | 0 minutes | 5 minutes | Easy |

**Servings**
1 person (For more people, multiply the ingredients by the number of people)

## INGREDIENTS:

- 1 large carrot, peeled and chopped (100 g)
- 1-inch piece fresh ginger, peeled and grated (10 g)
- 1 cup orange juice (240 ml)
- Pinch of cinnamon (American touch)
- Pinch of cardamom (British touch)

## PROCEDURE:

1. Combine chopped carrot, grated ginger, orange juice, cinnamon, and cardamom in a blender.
2. Blend until smooth.
3. Serve immediately.

## NUTRITIONAL VALUES:

- **Calories:** 150
- **Carbohydrates:** 36g
- **Proteins:** 2g
- **Fats:** 1g
- **Fiber:** 3g
- **Sodium:** 20mg
- **Glucose:** 30g
- **Cholesterol:** 0mg

## SUGGESTED SUBSTITUTIONS:

- Use apple juice instead of orange juice for a different flavor.
- Substitute cardamom with nutmeg for a spicier taste.

# Pear and Spinach Smoothie

| Preparation Time | Cooking Time | Total Time | Difficulty |
|---|---|---|---|
| 5 minutes | 0 minutes | 5 minutes | Easy |

**Servings**
1 person (For more people, multiply the ingredients by the number of people)

## INGREDIENTS:

- 1 ripe pear, peeled, cored, and chopped (150 g)
- 1 cup baby spinach (30 g)
- 1/2 cup filtered water (120 ml)
- 1 tbsp ground flax seeds (American touch) (15 g)
- Few fresh mint leaves (British touch)

## PROCEDURE:

1. Combine chopped pear, baby spinach, filtered water, and ground flax seeds in a blender.
2. Add fresh mint leaves.
3. Blend until smooth.
4. Serve immediately.

## NUTRITIONAL VALUES:

- **Calories:** 120
- **Carbohydrates:** 26g
- **Proteins:** 3g
- **Fats:** 2g
- **Fiber:** 7g
- **Sodium:** 50mg
- **Glucose:** 15g
- **Cholesterol:** 0mg

## SUGGESTED SUBSTITUTIONS:

- Substitute ground flax seeds with chia seeds.
- Replace mint leaves with basil for a different herbal note.

# Green Vegetable Juice

| Preparation Time | Cooking Time | Total Time | Difficulty |
|---|---|---|---|
| 5 minutes | 0 minutes | 5 minutes | Easy |

**Servings**
1 person (For more people, multiply the ingredients by the number of people)

## INGREDIENTS:

- 1 cucumber (150 g)
- 2 stalks celery (100 g)
- 1 green apple, cored and chopped (150 g)
- Handful of kale leaves (American touch)
- Handful of nettle leaves (British touch)

## PROCEDURE:

1. Wash and chop cucumber, celery, and green apple.
2. Pass them through a juicer.
3. For the American touch, add kale leaves while juicing.
4. For the British touch, add nettle leaves.
5. Stir well and serve immediately.

## NUTRITIONAL VALUES:

- **Calories:** 100
- **Carbohydrates:** 25g
- **Proteins:** 3g
- **Fats:** 1g
- **Fiber:** 6g
- **Sodium:** 150mg
- **Glucose:** 15g
- **Cholesterol:** 0mg

## SUGGESTED SUBSTITUTIONS:

- Use spinach instead of kale for a milder flavor.
- Substitute nettle with parsley for a different herbal addition.

# Avocado and Cucumber Smoothie

| Preparation Time | Cooking Time | Total Time | Difficulty |
|---|---|---|---|
| 5 minutes | 0 minutes | 5 minutes | Easy |

**Servings**
1 person (For more people, multiply the ingredients by the number of people)

## INGREDIENTS:

- 1 ripe avocado, peeled and pitted (150 g)
- 1/2 cucumber, peeled and chopped (100 g)
- 1/2 cup natural yogurt (120 ml)
- Juice of 1 lime (American touch)
- Few fresh mint leaves (British touch)

## PROCEDURE:

1. Combine avocado, chopped cucumber, natural yogurt, and lime juice in a blender.
2. Add fresh mint leaves.
3. Blend until smooth.
4. Serve immediately.

## NUTRITIONAL VALUES:

- **Calories:** 250
- **Carbohydrates:** 18g
- **Proteins:** 8g
- **Fats:** 17g
- **Fiber:** 9g
- **Sodium:** 50mg
- **Glucose:** 5g
- **Cholesterol:** 5mg

## SUGGESTED SUBSTITUTIONS:

- Replace lime juice with lemon juice.
- Use coconut milk instead of natural yogurt for a dairy-free option.

# Peach and Mango Smoothie

| Preparation Time | Cooking Time | Total Time | Difficulty |
|---|---|---|---|
| 5 minutes | 0 minutes | 5 minutes | Easy |

**Servings**
1 person (For more people, multiply the ingredients by the number of people)

## INGREDIENTS:

- 1 ripe peach, peeled and chopped (150 g)
- 1 ripe mango, peeled and chopped (200 g)
- 1 cup almond milk (240 ml)
- 1 tsp vanilla extract (American touch) (5 ml)
- 1 tbsp golden syrup (British touch) (15 ml)

## PROCEDURE:

1. Combine chopped peach, mango, almond milk, vanilla extract, and golden syrup in a blender.
2. Blend until smooth.
3. Serve immediately.

## NUTRITIONAL VALUES:

- **Calories:** 280
- **Carbohydrates:** 62g
- **Proteins:** 4g
- **Fats:** 3g
- **Fiber:** 8g
- **Sodium:** 100mg
- **Glucose:** 45g
- **Cholesterol:** 0mg

## SUGGESTED SUBSTITUTIONS:

- Use soy milk instead of almond milk.
- Substitute golden syrup with agave nectar for a lower glycemic option.

# Beet and Apple Juice

| Preparation Time | Cooking Time | Total Time | Difficulty |
|---|---|---|---|
| 5 minutes | 0 minutes | 5 minutes | Easy |

**Servings**
1 person (For more people, multiply the ingredients by the number of people)

## INGREDIENTS:

- 1 small beet, peeled and chopped (100 g)
- 1 red apple, cored and chopped (150 g)
- 1 carrot, peeled and chopped (75 g)
- 1-inch piece ginger, peeled and grated (American touch)
- Few basil leaves (British touch)

## PROCEDURE:

1. Pass chopped beet, apple, carrot, and grated ginger through a juicer.
2. For the American touch, include ginger while juicing.
3. For the British touch, add basil leaves.
4. Stir well and serve immediately.

## NUTRITIONAL VALUES:

- **Calories:** 120
- **Carbohydrates:** 28g
- **Proteins:** 2g
- **Fats:** 0g
- **Fiber:** 6g
- **Sodium:** 80mg
- **Glucose:** 20g
- **Cholesterol:** 0mg

## SUGGESTED SUBSTITUTIONS:

- Substitute basil with mint leaves for a different herbaceous flavor.
- Use lemon juice instead of ginger for a citrusy twist.

# Kiwi and Spinach Smoothie

| Preparation Time | Cooking Time | Total Time | Difficulty |
|---|---|---|---|
| 5 minutes | 0 minutes | 5 minutes | Easy |

**Servings**
1 person (For more people, multiply the ingredients by the number of people)

## INGREDIENTS:

- 2 kiwis, peeled and chopped (200 g)
- 1 cup spinach leaves (30 g)
- 1/2 cup coconut water (120 ml)
- 1 tbsp agave syrup (American touch) (15 ml)
- 1/2 tsp poppy seeds (British touch) (2 g)

## PROCEDURE:

1. Place chopped kiwis, spinach leaves, coconut water, agave syrup, and poppy seeds in a blender.
2. Blend until smooth.
3. Serve immediately.

## NUTRITIONAL VALUES:

- **Calories:** 180
- **Carbohydrates:** 42g
- **Proteins:** 4g
- **Fats:** 1g
- **Fiber:** 6g
- **Sodium:** 50mg
- **Glucose:** 30g
- **Cholesterol:** 0mg

## SUGGESTED SUBSTITUTIONS:

- Substitute agave syrup with honey for a different sweetness.
- Use chia seeds instead of poppy seeds for added texture.

# Blueberry and Yogurt Smoothie

| Preparation Time | Cooking Time | Total Time | Difficulty |
|---|---|---|---|
| 5 minutes | 0 minutes | 5 minutes | Easy |

**Servings**
1 person (For more people, multiply the ingredients by the number of people)

## INGREDIENTS:

- 1 cup blueberries (150 g)
- 1/2 cup natural yogurt (120 ml)
- 1/2 cup coconut milk (120 ml)
- 1/2 tsp vanilla extract (American touch) (2 ml)
- 1 tbsp maple syrup (British touch) (15 ml)

## PROCEDURE:

1. Combine blueberries, natural yogurt, coconut milk, vanilla extract, and maple syrup in a blender.
2. Blend until smooth.
3. Serve immediately.

## NUTRITIONAL VALUES:

- **Calories:** 220
- **Carbohydrates:** 38g
- **Proteins:** 5g
- **Fats:** 7g
- **Fiber:** 5g
- **Sodium:** 70mg
- **Glucose:** 25g
- **Cholesterol:** 10mg

## SUGGESTED SUBSTITUTIONS:

- Replace coconut milk with almond milk for a lighter option.
- Use honey instead of maple syrup for a different flavor profile

# Tomato and Carrot Juice

| Preparation Time | Cooking Time | Total Time | Difficulty |
|---|---|---|---|
| 5 minutes | 0 minutes | 5 minutes | Easy |

**Servings**
1 person (For more people, multiply the ingredients by the number of people)

## INGREDIENTS:

- 2 tomatoes, chopped (200 g)
- 1 large carrot, peeled and chopped (100 g)
- 1 stalk celery, chopped (50 g)
- Pinch of black pepper (American touch)
- Dash of Worcestershire sauce (British touch)

## PROCEDURE:

1. Pass chopped tomatoes, carrot, and celery through a juicer.
2. Add black pepper and Worcestershire sauce.
3. Stir well and serve immediately.

## NUTRITIONAL VALUES:

- **Calories:** 90
- **Carbohydrates:** 20g
- **Proteins:** 3g
- **Fats:** 1g
- **Fiber:** 5g
- **Sodium:** 150mg
- **Glucose:** 10g
- **Cholesterol:** 0mg

## SUGGESTED SUBSTITUTIONS:

- Substitute Worcestershire sauce with hot sauce for a spicier kick.
- Add a squeeze of lemon juice for a citrusy twist.

# Melon and Strawberry Smoothie

| Preparation Time | Cooking Time | Total Time | Difficulty |
|---|---|---|---|
| 5 minutes | 0 minutes | 5 minutes | Easy |

**Servings**
1 person (For more people, multiply the ingredients by the number of people)

## INGREDIENTS:

- 1 cup melon, chopped (150 g)
- 1/2 cup strawberries, hulled (75 g)
- 1/2 cup water (120 ml)
- Few fresh mint leaves (American touch)
- Pinch of dried lavender (British touch)

## PROCEDURE:

1. Combine chopped melon, strawberries, water, and fresh mint leaves in a blender.
2. Add dried lavender.
3. Blend until smooth.
4. Serve immediately.

## NUTRITIONAL VALUES:

- **Calories:** 100
- **Carbohydrates:** 24g
- **Proteins:** 2g
- **Fats:** 0g
- **Fiber:** 4g
- **Sodium:** 10mg
- **Glucose:** 20g
- **Cholesterol:** 0mg

## SUGGESTED SUBSTITUTIONS:

- Use basil leaves instead of mint for a different herbal note.
- Substitute dried lavender with rosemary for a unique flavor.

# Coconut and Pineapple Smoothie

| Preparation Time | Cooking Time | Total Time | Difficulty |
|---|---|---|---|
| 5 minutes | 0 minutes | 5 minutes | Easy |

**Servings**
1 person (For more people, multiply the ingredients by the number of people)

## INGREDIENTS:

- Flesh of 1 coconut, chopped (200 g)
- 1 cup pineapple chunks (150 g)
- 1/2 cup coconut water (120 ml)
- 1 tbsp coconut flakes (American touch) (15 g)
- Few fresh mint leaves (British touch)

## PROCEDURE:

1. Combine chopped coconut flesh, pineapple chunks, coconut water, and coconut flakes in a blender.
2. Add fresh mint leaves.
3. Blend until smooth.
4. Serve immediately.

## NUTRITIONAL VALUES:

- **Calories:** 280
- **Carbohydrates:** 40g
- **Proteins:** 3g
- **Fats:** 14g
- **Fiber:** 8g
- **Sodium:** 60mg
- **Glucose:** 25g
- **Cholesterol:** 0mg

## SUGGESTED SUBSTITUTIONS:

- Substitute coconut water with pineapple juice for added sweetness.
- Use toasted coconut chips instead of coconut flakes for a crunchy texture.

# Soft Foods

## Mashed Potatoes

| Preparation Time | Cooking Time | Total Time | Difficulty |
|---|---|---|---|
| 10 minutes | 20 minutes | 30 minutes | Easy |

**Servings**
1 person (For more people, multiply the ingredients by the number of people)

### INGREDIENTS:

- 2 medium potatoes, peeled and cubed (300 g)
- 2 tbsp butter (30 g)
- 1/4 cup milk (60 ml)
- 2 tbsp sour cream (American touch) (30 g)
- 1 tbsp chopped chives (British touch) (5 g)

### PROCEDURE:

1. Boil the peeled and cubed potatoes in salted water until tender, about 15-20 minutes.
2. Drain the potatoes and return them to the pot.
3. Add butter and mash until smooth.
4. Gradually add milk while mashing until desired consistency is reached.
5. Stir in sour cream and chopped chives.
6. Season with salt and pepper if desired.

### NUTRITIONAL VALUES:

- **Calories:** 400
- **Carbohydrates:** 50g
- **Proteins:** 6g
- **Fats:** 20g
- **Fiber:** 5g
- **Sodium:** 150mg
- **Glucose:** 10g
- **Cholesterol:** 50mg

### SUGGESTED SUBSTITUTIONS:

- Substitute sour cream with Greek yogurt for a healthier option.
- Use olive oil instead of butter for a dairy-free version.

## Steamed Carrots

| Preparation Time | Cooking Time | Total Time | Difficulty |
|---|---|---|---|
| 5 minutes | 10 minutes | 15 minutes | Easy |

**Servings**
1 person (For more people, multiply the ingredients by the number of people)

### INGREDIENTS:

- 2 medium carrots, peeled and sliced (150 g)
- Pinch of salt
- 1 tbsp honey (American touch) (15 ml)
- 1 tbsp chopped fresh parsley (British touch) (5 g)

### PROCEDURE:

1. Place sliced carrots in a steamer basket over boiling water.
2. Steam for about 8-10 minutes or until carrots are tender.
3. Remove from the steamer and transfer to a serving dish.
4. Drizzle honey over the carrots and sprinkle with chopped parsley.
5. Toss gently to coat evenly.
6. Serve warm.

### NUTRITIONAL VALUES:

- **Calories:** 120
- **Carbohydrates:** 28g
- **Proteins:** 2g
- **Fats:** 0g
- **Fiber:** 5g
- **Sodium:** 150mg
- **Glucose:** 20g
- **Cholesterol:** 0mg

### SUGGESTED SUBSTITUTIONS:

- Replace honey with maple syrup for a different sweetness.
- Use thyme instead of parsley for a herbaceous flavor.

# Baked Peeled Apples

| Preparation Time | Cooking Time | Total Time | Difficulty |
|---|---|---|---|
| 5 minutes | 30 minutes | 35 minutes | Easy |

**Servings**
1 person (For more people, multiply the ingredients by the number of people)

## INGREDIENTS:

- 2 apples, peeled and cored (300 g)
- 1/2 tsp cinnamon (2 g)
- 1 tbsp maple syrup (American touch) (15 ml)
- 1/4 tsp nutmeg (British touch) (1 g)

## PROCEDURE:

1. Preheat the oven to 350°F (175°C).
2. Place peeled and cored apples in a baking dish.
3. Sprinkle cinnamon and nutmeg over the apples.
4. Drizzle with maple syrup.
5. Bake for about 25-30 minutes or until the apples are tender.
6. Remove from the oven and let cool slightly before serving.

## NUTRITIONAL VALUES:

- **Calories:** 180
- **Carbohydrates:** 45g
- **Proteins:** 1g
- **Fats:** 0g
- **Fiber:** 8g
- **Sodium:** 0mg
- **Glucose:** 35g
- **Cholesterol:** 0mg

## SUGGESTED SUBSTITUTIONS:

- Use brown sugar instead of maple syrup for a richer flavor.
- Add a sprinkle of chopped walnuts for texture.

# Steamed Pumpkin with Olive Oil

| Preparation Time | Cooking Time | Total Time | Difficulty |
|---|---|---|---|
| 10 minutes | 20 minutes | 30 minutes | Easy |

**Servings**
1 person (For more people, multiply the ingredients by the number of people)

## INGREDIENTS:

- 1 cup pumpkin, peeled and cubed (150 g)
- 1 tbsp olive oil (15 ml)
- 1 tbsp toasted pumpkin seeds (American touch) (15 g)
- 1/2 tbsp fresh thyme leaves (British touch) (2 g)

## PROCEDURE:

1. Place cubed pumpkin in a steamer basket over boiling water.
2. Steam for about 15-20 minutes or until the pumpkin is tender.
3. Remove from the steamer and transfer to a serving dish.
4. Drizzle with olive oil.
5. Sprinkle it with toasted pumpkin seeds and fresh thyme leaves.
6. Serve warm.

## NUTRITIONAL VALUES:

- **Calories:** 180
- **Carbohydrates:** 10g
- **Proteins:** 2g
- **Fats:** 15g
- **Fiber:** 2g
- **Sodium:** 0mg
- **Glucose:** 5g
- **Cholesterol:** 0mg

## SUGGESTED SUBSTITUTIONS:

- Replace olive oil with melted butter for a different flavor.
- Use rosemary instead of thyme for an aromatic twist.

# Cauliflower Purée

| Preparation Time | Cooking Time | Total Time | Difficulty |
|---|---|---|---|
| 10 minutes | 15 minutes | 25 minutes | Easy |

**Servings**
1 person (For more people, multiply the ingredients by the number of people)

## INGREDIENTS:

- 1 small cauliflower head, chopped (300 g)
- 2 tbsp butter (30 g)
- 1/4 cup cream (60 ml)
- 2 tbsp grated cheddar cheese (American touch) (30 g)
- 1/2 tsp mild curry powder (British touch) (2 g)

## PROCEDURE:

1. Steam or boil chopped cauliflower until very tender, about 10-15 minutes.
2. Drain well and transfer cauliflower to a food processor.
3. Add butter and cream, then process until smooth.
4. Stir in grated cheddar cheese and mild curry powder.
5. Season with salt and pepper to taste.
6. Serve hot.

## NUTRITIONAL VALUES:

- **Calories:** 300
- **Carbohydrates:** 15g
- **Proteins:** 8g
- **Fats:** 25g
- **Fiber:** 5g
- **Sodium:** 150mg
- **Glucose:** 10g
- **Cholesterol:** 90mg

## SUGGESTED SUBSTITUTIONS:

- Substitute cream with coconut milk for a dairy-free option.
- Use garam masala instead of mild curry powder for a different spice blend.

# Baked Bananas with Honey and Cinnamon

| Preparation Time | Cooking Time | Total Time | Difficulty |
|---|---|---|---|
| 5 minutes | 20 minutes | 25 minutes | Easy |

**Servings**
1 person (For more people, multiply the ingredients by the number of people)

## INGREDIENTS:

- 2 ripe bananas, peeled and halved lengthwise (200 g)
- 2 tbsp honey (30 ml)
- 1/2 tsp cinnamon (2 g)
- 1 tbsp peanut butter (American touch) (15 g)
- 1 tbsp golden syrup (British touch) (15 ml)

## PROCEDURE:

1. Preheat the oven to 350°F (175°C).
2. Place banana halves in a baking dish.
3. Drizzle honey over the bananas.
4. Sprinkle with cinnamon.
5. Bake for about 15-20 minutes or until bananas are soft and caramelized.
6. Remove from the oven and let cool slightly.
7. Serve warm with a dollop of peanut butter and drizzle of golden syrup.

## NUTRITIONAL VALUES:

- **Calories:** 320
- **Carbohydrates:** 70g
- **Proteins:** 5g
- **Fats:** 7g
- **Fiber:** 6g
- **Sodium:** 5mg
- **Glucose:** 50g
- **Cholesterol:** 0mg

## SUGGESTED SUBSTITUTIONS:

- Substitute golden syrup with maple syrup for a different sweetness.
- Use almond butter instead of peanut butter for a nuttier flavor.

# Soft Roasted Sweet Potatoes

| **Preparation Time** | **Cooking Time** | **Total Time** | **Difficulty** |
|---|---|---|---|
| 10 minutes | 30 minutes | 40 minutes | Easy |

**Servings**
1 person (For more people, multiply the ingredients by the number of people)

## INGREDIENTS:

- 1 medium sweet potato, peeled and cubed (200 g)
- 1 tbsp olive oil (15 ml)
- 2 tbsp mini marshmallows (American touch) (15 g)
- 1/2 tsp ground ginger (British touch) (2 g)

## PROCEDURE:

1. Preheat the oven to 400°F (200°C).
2. Toss cubed sweet potato with olive oil, ground ginger, and a pinch of salt.
3. Spread sweet potato cubes in a single layer on a baking sheet.
4. Roast for about 25-30 minutes or until tender and caramelized, flipping halfway through.
5. Remove from the oven and sprinkle mini marshmallows over the sweet potatoes.
6. Return to the oven and broil for 1-2 minutes until marshmallows are lightly toasted.
7. Serve hot.

## NUTRITIONAL VALUES:

- **Calories:** 300
- **Carbohydrates:** 60g
- **Proteins:** 4g
- **Fats:** 5g
- **Fiber:** 8g
- **Sodium:** 50mg
- **Glucose:** 30g
- **Cholesterol:** 0mg

## SUGGESTED SUBSTITUTIONS:

- Use cinnamon instead of ground ginger for a different spice profile.
- Substitute mini marshmallows with chopped pecans for added crunch.

## Breakfast

# Oat Porridge with Banana and Maple Syrup

| Preparation Time | Cooking Time | Total Time | Difficulty |
|---|---|---|---|
| 5 minutes | 10 minutes | 15 minutes | Easy |

**Servings**
1 person (For more people, multiply the ingredients by the number of people)

### INGREDIENTS:

- 1/2 cup oats (50 g)
- 1 cup water or non-dairy milk (240 ml)
- 1/2 banana, sliced (American touch)
- 1 tbsp pure maple syrup (American touch) (15 ml)
- Pinch of nutmeg (British touch)

### PROCEDURE:

1. In a small saucepan, bring water or non-dairy milk to a boil.
2. Stir in oats and reduce heat to low. Cook for about 5-7 minutes, stirring occasionally, until oats are thick and creamy.
3. Remove from heat and let stand for 1-2 minutes.
4. Transfer oat porridge to a bowl.
5. Top with sliced banana, drizzle with pure maple syrup, and sprinkle with nutmeg.
6. Serve warm.

### NUTRITIONAL VALUES:

- **Calories:** 300
- **Carbohydrates:** 60g
- **Proteins:** 6g
- **Fats:** 4g
- **Fiber:** 8g
- **Sodium:** 50mg
- **Glucose:** 30g
- **Cholesterol:** 0mg

### SUGGESTED SUBSTITUTIONS:

- Substitute maple syrup with honey for a different sweetness.
- Use cinnamon instead of nutmeg for a warm spice flavor.

# Papaya Smoothie with Yogurt and Manuka Honey

| Preparation Time | Cooking Time | Total Time | Difficulty |
|---|---|---|---|
| 5 minutes | 0 minutes | 5 minutes | Easy |

**Servings**
1 person (For more people, multiply the ingredients by the number of people)

### INGREDIENTS:

- 1 cup fresh papaya, cubed (150 g)
- 1/2 cup Greek or coconut yogurt (120 g)
- 1 tbsp Manuka honey (British touch) (15 ml)
- 1/2 tsp cinnamon or vanilla extract (American touch) (2 ml)

### PROCEDURE:

1. In a blender, combine fresh papaya and yogurt.
2. Add Manuka honey and cinnamon or vanilla extract.
3. Blend until smooth and creamy.
4. Pour into a glass and serve immediately.

### NUTRITIONAL VALUES:

- **Calories:** 250
- **Carbohydrates:** 45g
- **Proteins:** 10g
- **Fats:** 5g
- **Fiber:** 5g
- **Sodium:** 50mg
- **Glucose:** 35g
- **Cholesterol:** 5mg

### SUGGESTED SUBSTITUTIONS:

- Use regular honey if Manuka honey is not available.
- Substitute papaya with mango for a tropical variation

# Spinach, Mushroom, and Cheddar Omelet

| Preparation Time | Cooking Time | Total Time | Difficulty |
|:---:|:---:|:---:|:---:|
| 10 minutes | 10 minutes | 20 minutes | Easy |

**Servings**
1 person (For more people, multiply the ingredients by the number of people)

## INGREDIENTS:

- 2 eggs
- 1/2 cup spinach, chopped (30 g)
- 1/4 cup mushrooms, sliced (30 g)
- 1/4 cup grated cheddar cheese (British touch) (30 g)
- Spicy ketchup (American touch), to taste

## PROCEDURE:

1. In a bowl, beat eggs until well mixed.
2. Heat a non-stick skillet over medium heat.
3. Add spinach and mushrooms to the skillet and sauté for 2-3 minutes until spinach is wilted and mushrooms are tender.
4. Pour beaten eggs over the spinach and mushrooms.
5. Cook the omelet for 3-4 minutes or until the edges start to set.
6. Sprinkle grated cheddar cheese over half of the omelet.
7. Fold the omelet in half and cook for another 1-2 minutes until cheese is melted and eggs are cooked through.
8. Slide the omelet onto a plate, garnish with spicy ketchup, and serve hot.

## NUTRITIONAL VALUES:

- **Calories:** 350
- **Carbohydrates:** 5g
- **Proteins:** 25g
- **Fats:** 25g
- **Fiber:** 2g
- **Sodium:** 400mg
- **Glucose:** 2g
- **Cholesterol:** 450mg

## SUGGESTED SUBSTITUTIONS:

- Use feta cheese instead of cheddar for a tangier flavor.
- Replace spicy ketchup with salsa for a different kick.

# Banana and Oat Pancakes with Jam

| Preparation Time | Cooking Time | Total Time | Difficulty |
|---|---|---|---|
| 10 minutes | 10 minutes | 20 minutes | Easy |

**Servings**
1 person (For more people, multiply the ingredients by the number of people)

## INGREDIENTS:
- 1 ripe banana, mashed
- 1/2 cup ground oats (50 g)
- Berry jam (British touch), to taste
- Maple syrup (American touch), to taste

## PROCEDURE:
1. In a bowl, mash the ripe banana until smooth.
2. Add ground oats to the mashed banana and mix well to form a batter.
3. Heat a non-stick skillet or griddle over medium heat.
4. Spoon the batter onto the skillet to form pancakes of desired size.
5. Cook for 2-3 minutes until bubbles form on the surface.
6. Flip the pancakes and cook for another 1-2 minutes until golden brown and cooked through.
7. Serve the pancakes topped with berry jam and a drizzle of maple syrup.

## NUTRITIONAL VALUES:
- **Calories:** 300
- **Carbohydrates:** 60g
- **Proteins:** 5g
- **Fats:** 3g
- **Fiber:** 6g
- **Sodium:** 100mg
- **Glucose:** 35g
- **Cholesterol:** 0mg

## SUGGESTED SUBSTITUTIONS:
- Use honey instead of maple syrup for a different sweetness.
- Substitute ground oats with almond flour for a gluten-free option

# Whole Grain Toast with Avocado and Baked Beans

| Preparation Time | Cooking Time | Total Time | Difficulty |
|---|---|---|---|
| 5 minutes | 5 minutes | 10 minutes | Easy |

**Servings**
1 person (For more people, multiply the ingredients by the number of people)

## INGREDIENTS:
- 1 slice whole grain bread
- 1/2 avocado, mashed
- Baked beans (British touch), warmed
- Crispy beef bacon (American touch), optional

## PROCEDURE:
1. Toast the whole grain bread until golden brown.
2. Spread mashed avocado evenly over the toasted bread slice.
3. Heat the baked beans in a small saucepan or microwave until warmed through.
4. Spoon the warmed baked beans over the avocado toast.
5. If desired, top with crispy bacon for an additional flavor.

## NUTRITIONAL VALUES:
- **Calories:** 350
- **Carbohydrates:** 45g
- **Proteins:** 15g
- **Fats:** 12g
- **Fiber:** 12g
- **Sodium:** 600mg
- **Glucose:** 15g
- **Cholesterol:** 10mg

## SUGGESTED SUBSTITUTIONS:
- Use guacamole instead of mashed avocado for added spice.
- Substitute baked beans with refried beans for a different texture.

# Chia Pudding with Almond Milk and Berry Compote

| Preparation Time | Cooking Time | Total Time | Difficulty |
|---|---|---|---|
| 5 minutes (+ soaking time) | 0 minutes | 5 minutes (+ soaking time) | Easy |

**Servings**
1 person (For more people, multiply the ingredients by the number of people)

## INGREDIENTS:

- 1/4 cup chia seeds (40 g)
- 1 cup almond milk (240 ml)
- Berry compote (British touch), to taste
- Almond butter or chopped pecans (American touch), for garnish

## PROCEDURE:

1. In a bowl or jar, combine chia seeds and almond milk.
2. Stir well to combine. Let the mixture sit for 5 minutes, then stir again to prevent clumping.
3. Cover and refrigerate for at least 2 hours or overnight to allow the chia seeds to absorb the almond milk and thicken.
4. Once thickened, stir the chia pudding again. If desired, add more almond milk to reach the desired consistency.
5. Top with berry compote and garnish with almond butter or chopped pecans.

## NUTRITIONAL VALUES:

- **Calories:** 300
- **Carbohydrates:** 30g
- **Proteins:** 10g
- **Fats:** 15g
- **Fiber:** 15g
- **Sodium:** 150mg
- **Glucose:** 10g
- **Cholesterol:** 0mg

## SUGGESTED SUBSTITUTIONS:

- Use coconut milk instead of almond milk for a richer flavor.
- Substitute berry compote with fresh berries for a different texture.

# Sweet Potato and Carrot Soup with Beef Bacon

| Preparation Time | Cooking Time | Total Time | Difficulty |
|---|---|---|---|
| 10 minutes | 20 minutes | 30 minutes | Easy |

**Servings**
1 person (For more people, multiply the ingredients by the number of people)

## INGREDIENTS:

- 1 small sweet potato, peeled and diced
- 2 carrots, peeled and sliced
- 2 cups water or vegetable broth (480 ml)
- Crispy beef bacon (American touch), chopped
- Buttered whole grain bread (British touch), for serving

## PROCEDURE:

1. In a medium pot, combine sweet potato, carrots, and water or vegetable broth.
2. Bring to a boil over medium-high heat, then reduce heat to low. Simmer for 15-20 minutes, or until vegetables are tender.
3. Remove from heat and let cool slightly.
4. Using an immersion blender or regular blender, blend the soup until smooth.
5. If needed, return the soup to the pot and reheat over low heat until warmed through.
6. Serve the soup hot, garnished with crispy chopped bacon.
7. Serve with buttered whole grain bread on the side.

## NUTRITIONAL VALUES:

- **Calories:** 300
- **Carbohydrates:** 40g
- **Proteins:** 8g
- **Fats:** 12g
- **Fiber:** 8g
- **Sodium:** 500mg
- **Glucose:** 15g
- **Cholesterol:** 20mg

## SUGGESTED SUBSTITUTIONS:

- Use turkey bacon instead of regular beef bacon for a lighter option.
- Substitute sweet potato with butternut squash for a similar texture.

# Introduction to Fiber

## Lentil and Barley Soup

| Preparation Time | Cooking Time | Total Time | Difficulty |
|---|---|---|---|
| 10 minutes | 30 minutes | 40 minutes | Easy |

**Servings**
1 person (For more people, multiply the ingredients by the number of people)

### INGREDIENTS:

- 1/4 cup lentils, rinsed (50 g)
- 1/4 cup whole barley (50 g) (British touch)
- 1 carrot, diced
- 1 celery stalk, diced
- 1 cup vegetable broth (240 ml)
- Sweet and smoky barbecue sauce (American touch)

### PROCEDURE:

1. In a medium pot, combine lentils, barley, carrot, celery, and vegetable broth.
2. Bring to a boil over medium-high heat, then reduce heat to low and simmer for 30 minutes, or until lentils and barley are tender.
3. Stir in sweet and smoky barbecue sauce to taste.
4. Remove from heat and let it sit for a few minutes before serving.

### NUTRITIONAL VALUES:

- **Calories:** 320
- **Carbohydrates:** 60g
- **Proteins:** 15g
- **Fats:** 2g
- **Fiber:** 12g
- **Sodium:** 650mg
- **Glucose:** 10g
- **Cholesterol:** 0mg

### SUGGESTED SUBSTITUTIONS:

1. Substitute quinoa for barley.
2. Use diced potatoes instead of carrots.

## Warm Quinoa and Roasted Squash Salad

| Preparation Time | Cooking Time | Total Time | Difficulty |
|---|---|---|---|
| 15 minutes | 25 minutes | 40 minutes | Easy |

**Servings**
1 person (For more people, multiply the ingredients by the number of people)

### INGREDIENTS:

- 1/2 cup quinoa, cooked (90 g) (American touch)
- 1 cup roasted squash, cubed
- 2 tbsp toasted pumpkin seeds (British touch)
- Olive oil, for drizzling
- Juice of 1/2 lemon

### PROCEDURE:

1. Cook quinoa according to package instructions. Fluff with a fork and set aside.
2. Preheat the oven to 400°F (200°C).
3. Toss cubed squash with olive oil and spread on a baking sheet. Roast for 20-25 minutes until tender and slightly caramelized.
4. In a serving bowl, combine cooked quinoa and roasted squash.
5. Drizzle with olive oil and lemon juice.
6. Sprinkle toasted pumpkin seeds on top.
7. Serve warm.

### NUTRITIONAL VALUES:

- **Calories:** 380
- **Carbohydrates:** 55g
- **Proteins:** 10g
- **Fats:** 15g
- **Fiber:** 10g
- **Sodium:** 20mg
- **Glucose:** 8g
- **Cholesterol:** 0mg

### SUGGESTED SUBSTITUTIONS:

3. Substitute sweet potatoes for squash.
4. Use sunflower seeds instead of pumpkin seeds.

# Mushroom Risotto with Herbs

| Preparation Time | Cooking Time | Total Time | Difficulty |
|---|---|---|---|
| 15 minutes | 30 minutes | 45 minutes | Easy |

**Servings**
1 person (For more people, multiply the ingredients by the number of people)

## INGREDIENTS:

- 1/2 cup brown rice, uncooked (90 g) (American touch)
- 1 cup champignon mushrooms, sliced
- Fresh thyme and rosemary (British touch)
- Olive oil
- Vegetable broth, as needed

## PROCEDURE:

1. In a medium pan, heat olive oil over medium heat. Add mushrooms and sauté until golden brown, about 5-7 minutes.
2. Add brown rice to the pan and toast for 2 minutes, stirring frequently.
3. Gradually add vegetable broth, 1/2 cup at a time, stirring constantly until absorbed. Continue this process until the rice is cooked through and creamy, about 25-30 minutes.
4. Stir in fresh thyme and rosemary during the last 5 minutes of cooking.
5. Remove from heat and let it rest for a few minutes before serving.

## NUTRITIONAL VALUES:

- **Calories:** 400
- **Carbohydrates:** 75g
- **Proteins:** 8g
- **Fats:** 7g
- **Fiber:** 6g
- **Sodium:** 450mg
- **Glucose:** 12g
- **Cholesterol:** 0mg

## SUGGESTED SUBSTITUTIONS:

- Use Arborio rice instead of brown rice.
- Replace champignon mushrooms with shiitake mushrooms

# Vegetable Chili with Black Beans

| Preparation Time | Cooking Time | Total Time | Difficulty |
|---|---|---|---|
| 15 minutes | 25 minutes | 40 minutes | Easy |

**Servings**
1 person (For more people, multiply the ingredients by the number of people)

## INGREDIENTS:

- 1/2 cup black beans, cooked (100 g)
- 1 bell pepper, diced
- 1 small zucchini, diced
- Grated cheddar cheese (British touch)
- Tortilla chips (American touch)

## PROCEDURE:

1. In a medium pot, combine black beans, bell pepper, zucchini, and enough water to cover.
2. Bring to a boil over medium-high heat, then reduce heat and simmer for 20 minutes, or until vegetables are tender.
3. Season with salt and pepper to taste.
4. Serve topped with grated cheddar cheese and a side of tortilla chips.

## NUTRITIONAL VALUES:

- **Calories:** 350
- **Carbohydrates:** 55g
- **Proteins:** 15g
- **Fats:** 10g
- **Fiber:** 12g
- **Sodium:** 600mg
- **Glucose:** 10g
- **Cholesterol:** 15mg

## SUGGESTED SUBSTITUTIONS:

- Substitute kidney beans for black beans.
- Use mozzarella cheese instead of cheddar.

# Whole Grain Pasta with Spinach Pesto

| Preparation Time | Cooking Time | Total Time | Difficulty |
|---|---|---|---|
| 10 minutes | 15 minutes | 25 minutes | Easy |

**Servings**
1 person (For more people, multiply the ingredients by the number of people)

## INGREDIENTS:

- 1 cup whole grain pasta, uncooked (120 g)
- Fresh spinach and nut pesto (American touch)
- Cooked sweet peas (British touch)

## PROCEDURE:

1. Cook whole grain pasta according to package instructions. Drain and set aside.
2. In a blender or food processor, blend fresh spinach and nut pesto until smooth.
3. Toss cooked pasta with spinach pesto until well coated.
4. Gently fold in cooked sweet peas.
5. Serve warm.

## NUTRITIONAL VALUES:

- **Calories:** 420
- **Carbohydrates:** 65g
- **Proteins:** 15g
- **Fats:** 12g
- **Fiber:** 10g
- **Sodium:** 280mg
- **Glucose:** 8g
- **Cholesterol:** 0mg

## SUGGESTED SUBSTITUTIONS:

- Use basil pesto instead of spinach pesto.
- Substitute broccoli for sweet peas.

# Sweet Potato and Lentil Casserole

| Preparation Time | Cooking Time | Total Time | Difficulty |
|---|---|---|---|
| 15 minutes | 40 minutes | 55 minutes | Easy |

**Servings**
1 person (For more people, multiply the ingredients by the number of people)

## INGREDIENTS:

- 1 sweet potato, peeled and diced
- 1/2 cup lentils, cooked (100 g)
- Crispy beef bacon (American touch)
- Cooked applesauce (British touch)

## PROCEDURE:

1. Preheat the oven to 375°F (190°C).
2. In a baking dish, layer diced sweet potato and cooked lentils.
3. Cover with foil and bake for 30-35 minutes, or until sweet potatoes are tender.
4. Remove foil and bake for an additional 10 minutes to crisp up the top.
5. Serve hot, topped with crispy bacon and a dollop of cooked applesauce.

## NUTRITIONAL VALUES:

- **Calories:** 380
- **Carbohydrates:** 60g
- **Proteins:** 15g
- **Fats:** 8g
- **Fiber:** 12g
- **Sodium:** 400mg
- **Glucose:** 10g
- **Cholesterol:** 10mg

## SUGGESTED SUBSTITUTIONS:

- Use butternut squash instead of sweet potato.
- Replace beef bacon with toasted almonds.

# Couscous with Roasted Vegetables and Hummus

| Preparation Time | Cooking Time | Total Time | Difficulty |
|---|---|---|---|
| 10 minutes | 20 minutes | 30 minutes | Easy |

**Servings**
1 person (For more people, multiply the ingredients by the number of people)

## INGREDIENTS:

- 1/2 cup whole grain couscous (90 g)
- Roasted vegetables (eggplant, bell peppers), diced
- Hummus (American touch)
- Olive oil, for drizzling (British touch)

## PROCEDURE:

1. Cook the couscous according to package instructions. Typically, boil water (about 1 cup), remove from heat, add couscous, cover, and let sit for 5 minutes. Fluff with a fork.
2. While the couscous cooks, roast the vegetables in a preheated oven at 400°F (200°C) for 15-20 minutes or until tender.
3. Fluff the couscous with a fork and transfer to a serving bowl.
4. Top with roasted vegetables.
5. Drizzle with olive oil and add dollops of hummus on top.
6. Serve warm.

## NUTRITIONAL VALUES:

- **Calories:** 360
- **Carbohydrates:** 65g
- **Proteins:** 10g
- **Fats:** 7g
- **Fiber:** 8g
- **Sodium:** 350mg
- **Glucose:** 10g
- **Cholesterol:** 0mg

## SUGGESTED SUBSTITUTIONS:

- Substitute quinoa or bulgur for couscous.
- Use tahini sauce instead of hummus for a different flavor.

# Part 3

# MEAL PLANS

# BONUS 1 - Weekly Meal Plan for Diverticulitis During Flare-Up Phase

| DAY | BREAKFAST | SNACK | LUNCH | DINNER |
|---|---|---|---|---|
| **Monday** | Clear Chicken Broth | Coconut water | Clear chicken soup | Clear turkey broth |
| **Tuesday** | Sugar Free jelly | Clear beef broth | Carrots cream | Fennel cream |
| **Wednesday** | Clear vegetable broth | White cranberry juice | Clear beef broth | Chicken broth with herbs |
| **Thursday** | Weak green tea | Clear vegetable broth | Courgette cream | Pumpkin cream |
| **Friday** | Rice water | Pear juice | Clear vegetable soup | Light vegetable soup |
| **Saturday** | Clear chicken broth | Chamomile tea | Potatoes cream | Beef broth with herbs |
| **Sunday** | Sugar free gelatine | Clear fish broth | Clear fish soup | Celery cream |

# BONUS 2 - Weekly Meal Plan for Diverticulitis During Acute Phase

| DAY | BREAKFAST | SNACK | LUNCH | AFTERNOON SNACK | DINNER |
|---|---|---|---|---|---|
| **Monday** | Rice Porridge with maple syrup (American touch) and blackcurrant jam (British touch) | Natural Apple Jelly with whipped cream (American touch) | Potato and Leek Soup with dill (American touch) and chopped parsley (British touch) | Natural Yogurt with acacia honey (American touch) | Mashed Potatoes with sour cream (American touch) and chopped chives (British touch) |
| **Tuesday** | Banana and Yogurt Smoothie with extra banana (American touch) and eucalyptus honey (British touch) | Applesauce with cinnamon (American touch) | Clear Turkey Consommé with sage leaves (American touch) and fennel seeds (British touch) | Mashed Bananas with peanut butter (American touch) and golden syrup (British touch) | Steamed Carrots with honey (American touch) and chopped fresh parsley (British touch) |

| DAY | BREAKFAST | SNACK | LUNCH | AFTERNOON SNACK | DINNER |
|---|---|---|---|---|---|
| **Wednesday** | Oatmeal Cream with honey (American touch) and apple compote (British touch) | Rice Pudding with dried blueberries (American touch) and Demerara sugar (British touch) | Light Beet Soup with sour cream (American touch) and ground cumin (British touch) | Pear and Apple Smoothie with vanilla (American touch) and ground cinnamon (British touch) | Steamed Pumpkin with Olive Oil, toasted pumpkin seeds (American touch) and fresh thyme (British touch) |
| **Thursday** | Potato Pancakes with maple syrup (American touch) and applesauce (British touch) | Kiwi and Spinach Smoothie with agave syrup (American touch) and poppy seeds (British touch) | Delicate Beef Broth with garlic powder (American touch) and cloves (British touch) | Avocado and Cucumber Smoothie with lime (American touch) and fresh mint (British touch) | Cauliflower Purée with grated cheddar cheese (American touch) and mild curry powder (British touch) |
| **Friday** | Soft Scrambled Eggs on Toast with scrambled eggs (American touch) and extra white toast (British touch) | Coconut and Pineapple Smoothie with coconut flakes (American touch) and mint leaves (British touch) | Pumpkin and Carrot Soup with cinnamon (American touch) and fresh ginger (British touch) | Melon and Strawberry Smoothie with mint (American touch) and lavender (British touch) | Baked Bananas with Honey and Cinnamon with peanut butter (American touch) and golden syrup (British touch) |
| **Saturday** | Tapioca Pudding with whipped cream (American touch) and vanilla extract (British touch) | Tomato and Carrot Juice with black pepper (American touch) and Worcestershire sauce (British touch) | Light Chicken Soup with thyme (American touch) and rosemary (British touch) | Green Vegetable Juice with kale (American touch) and nettle (British touch) | Soft Roasted Sweet Potatoes with mini marshmallows (American touch) and ground ginger (British touch) |
| **Sunday** | Blueberry Jelly with whipped cream (American touch) and extra blueberries (British touch) | Peach and Mango Smoothie with vanilla (American touch) and golden syrup (British touch) | Light Fish Broth with fresh cilantro (American touch) and lemon extract (British touch) | Beet and Apple Juice with ginger (American touch) and basil leaves (British touch) | Baked Peeled Apples with maple syrup (American touch) and nutmeg (British touch) |

This meal plan provides variety and nutrition, keeping the food intake gentle during the acute phase of diverticulitis, with both American and British touches to make meals more interesting and satisfying.

# BONUS 3 - Weekly Meal Plan for Diverticulitis in Remission Phase

This meal plan is designed to help you manage your daily diet, ensuring you receive balanced nutrition while adhering to the dietary guidelines suitable for the remission phase of diverticulitis.

| DAY | BREAKFAST | SNACK | LUNCH | AFTER-NOON SNACK | DINNER | DESSERT |
|---|---|---|---|---|---|---|
| **Monday** | Oat porridge with banana and maple syrup (American touch) and nutmeg (British touch) | Greek yogurt (American touch) with Manuka honey (British touch) and granola | Barley and vegetable soup with beef bacon (American touch) or with buttered toast (British touch) | Hummus with baby carrots and celery (American touch) or with curry powder (British touch) | Steamed chicken with vegetables and Worcestershire sauce. Zucchini and carrots (American touch), Worcestershire sauce (British touch) | Vanilla panna cotta with strawberry sauce (American touch: vanilla pods, British touch: fresh strawberry sauce) |
| **Tuesday** | Papaya smoothie with yogurt and Manuka honey (American touch: cinnamon or vanilla, British touch: Manuka honey) | Oat cookies with apple and cinnamon (American touch: cinnamon, British touch: cooked apple pieces) | Couscous with roasted vegetables and hummus (American touch: hummus, British touch: fresh parsley) | Whole grain toast with avocado (American touch: light ranch dressing, British touch: whole grain bread) | Asparagus and lemon risotto (American touch: lemon zest, British touch: Parmesan cheese) | Rice pudding with honey and cinnamon (American touch: cinnamon, British touch: honey) |
| **Wednesday** | Spinach, mushroom, and cheddar omelet (American touch: spicy ketchup, British touch: grated cheddar) | Mini banana and date muffins (American touch: chopped dates, British touch: nutmeg) | Vegetable chili with black beans (American touch: tortilla chips, British touch: grated cheddar) | Butter and sea salt popcorn (American touch: clarified butter, British touch: sea salt) | Baked salmon with mustard and honey (American touch: honey, British touch: buttered sweet peas) | Blueberry jelly with whipped cream (American touch: natural gelatin, British touch: fresh whipped cream) |

| DAY | BREAKFAST | SNACK | LUNCH | AFTER-NOON SNACK | DINNER | DESSERT |
|---|---|---|---|---|---|---|
| **Thursday** | Banana and oat pancakes with jam (American touch: maple syrup, British touch: berry jam) | Whole grain toast with avocado (American touch: light ranch dressing, British touch: whole grain bread) | Warm quinoa and roasted squash salad (American touch: cooked quinoa, British touch: toasted pumpkin seeds) | Chia pudding with almond milk and berry compote (American touch: almond milk, British touch: berry compote) | Vegetable minestrone with beef chunks (American touch: beef chunks, British touch: buttered whole grain croutons) | Lemon sorbet with crumbled shortbread cookies (American touch: shortbread cookies, British touch: lemon sorbet) |
| **Friday** | Whole grain toast with avocado and baked beans (American touch: crispy beef bacon, British touch: baked beans) | Hummus with baby carrots and celery (American touch: baby carrots and celery, British touch: curry powder) | Whole grain pasta with spinach pesto (American touch: fresh spinach and nut pesto, British touch: cooked sweet peas) | Oat cookies with apple and cinnamon (American touch: cinnamon, British touch: cooked apple pieces) | Wild rice casserole with chicken and celery (American touch: diced chicken, British touch: cream of mushroom) | Yogurt and honey cups with pecans (American touch: toasted pecans, British touch: honey) |
| **Saturday** | Chia pudding with almond milk and berry compote (American touch: almond milk, British touch: berry compote) | Greek yogurt with Manuka honey and granola (American touch: Greek yogurt, British touch: Manuka honey) | Barley bowl with edamame beans and avocado (American touch: edamame beans, British touch: tahini sauce) | Mini banana and date muffins (American touch: chopped dates, British touch: nutmeg) | Roast chicken with applesauce (American touch: barbecue spices, British touch: reduced apple sauce) | Mango mousse with lime zest (American touch: mango pulp, British touch: lime zest) |

| DAY | BREAKFAST | SNACK | LUNCH | AFTER-NOON SNACK | DINNER | DESSERT |
|------|-----------|-------|-------|------------------|--------|---------|
| **Sunday** | Sweet potato and carrot soup with beef bacon (American touch: crispy beef bacon, British touch: buttered whole grain bread) | Butter and sea salt popcorn (American touch: clarified butter, British touch: sea salt) | Mushroom risotto with herbs (American touch: brown rice, British touch: fresh thyme and rosemary) | Whole grain toast with avocado (American touch: light ranch dressing, British touch: whole grain bread) | Curry tofu with basmati rice (American touch: fresh cilantro, British touch: basmati rice) | Gluten-free apple crumble (American touch: vanilla ice cream, British touch: gluten-free oat flour) |

## General Tips

- Drink plenty of water every day to aid digestion.
- Introduce new foods gradually and monitor how your body reacts.
- Avoid foods you know are irritating during remission periods.
- Consult your doctor or dietitian before making significant changes to your diet.

# FAQS

## 1. How does a healthy diet help me manage my diverticulitis?

**Answer**: A healthy diet plays a crucial role in managing diverticulitis by reducing inflammation, promoting regular bowel movements, and preventing flare-ups. It typically involves high-fiber foods during remission phases to maintain colon health and clear liquid or low-residue foods during flare-ups and acute phases to minimize irritation. This dietary approach supports overall digestive function and helps in symptom management.

## 2. Can I eat foods with high sodium at any phase of diverticulitis?

**Answer**: It's generally advisable to limit foods high in sodium throughout all phases of diverticulitis. High sodium intake can lead to fluid retention and potentially worsen symptoms like bloating and discomfort. During flare-ups and acute phases, especially when the digestive system is sensitive, opting for low-sodium alternatives can be beneficial for managing symptoms.

## 3. How can I maintain a healthy lifestyle while busy taking medication for diverticulitis?

**Answer**: Maintaining a healthy lifestyle while managing diverticulitis and taking medication involves planning and prioritizing self-care. This includes following a balanced diet as recommended in the specific phases of the condition, staying hydrated, getting regular exercise as advised by your healthcare provider, managing stress through relaxation techniques or mindfulness practices, and ensuring consistent medication adherence as prescribed.

## 4. How long should I follow the meal plan provided?

**Answer**: The duration of following a meal plan for diverticulitis can vary depending on individual health status and the phase of the condition. Generally, during flare-ups and acute phases, specific dietary restrictions may be necessary until symptoms improve. In remission phases, transitioning to a high-fiber diet and maintaining it long-term can help prevent recurrence of symptoms. It's essential to consult with your healthcare provider to tailor the meal plan to your specific needs.

## 5. Can my doctor recommend these recipes too?

**Answer**: Yes, healthcare providers can recommend dietary guidelines and recipes tailored to manage diverticulitis effectively. They consider individual health conditions, medication interactions, and dietary preferences to ensure that the recommended recipes align with your treatment plan. Collaboration with a healthcare provider ensures that dietary choices support overall health and symptom management.

## 6. What happens if I have allergies?

**Answer**: If you have allergies, it's crucial to carefully review all ingredients and adapt recipes accordingly. Allergic reactions can exacerbate symptoms and complicate the management of diverticulitis. Communicate any food allergies or intolerances to your healthcare provider and consider working with a registered dietitian to modify recipes while ensuring nutritional adequacy. Always prioritize safety and avoid consuming foods that trigger allergic reactions.

## 7. What are the benefits of a high-fiber diet for diverticulitis?

**Answer**: A high-fiber diet helps maintain regular bowel movements and reduces pressure in the colon, lowering the risk of diverticula formation and inflammation. It also promotes overall digestive health by supporting beneficial gut bacteria.

A high-fiber diet is beneficial for diverticulitis as it promotes regular bowel movements, reduces pressure on the colon, and supports overall digestive health. Fiber helps soften stool, making it easier to pass, which can alleviate symptoms such as constipation or diarrhea associated with the condition. Moreover, fiber-rich foods like fruits, vegetables, whole grains, and legumes provide essential nutrients and contribute to a balanced diet.

## 8. What should I do if I experience a flare-up despite following a recommended diet?

**Answer**: Flare-ups can occur despite following dietary guidelines. During a flare-up, it's essential to revert to a clear liquid diet initially and gradually reintroduce low-fiber foods as symptoms improve. Contact your healthcare provider for guidance on managing symptoms and adjusting your diet plan if necessary.

Despite following a recommended diet, flare-ups of diverticulitis can still occur. During a flare-up, it's crucial to prioritize rest and hydration while transitioning to a clear liquid diet to allow your digestive system to recover. As symptoms improve, slowly reintroduce low-fiber foods like plain rice, broth, and cooked fruits. Consult your healthcare provider for personalized advice and possible adjustments to your diet plan to manage symptoms effectively.

## 9. Are there specific supplements that can support my digestive health with diverticulitis?

**Answer**: While dietary adjustments are essential, supplements such as probiotics and psyllium husk may support digestive health in individuals with diverticulitis. Probiotics help maintain a healthy balance of gut bacteria, while psyllium husk, a soluble fiber supplement, can aid in regulating bowel movements.

Probiotics and psyllium husk are supplements that can support digestive health in individuals with diverticulitis. Probiotics help maintain a healthy balance of beneficial gut bacteria, which is crucial for overall digestive function and immune health. Psyllium husk, a soluble fiber supplement, can aid in regulating bowel movements by adding bulk to stool and promoting regularity. Before starting any supplements, consult your healthcare provider to ensure they are appropriate for your condition and do not interact with any medications you may be taking.

## 10. Can stress or emotional factors affect my diverticulitis symptoms?

**Answer**: Stress and emotional factors can exacerbate symptoms of diverticulitis. Stress management techniques such as yoga, meditation, and deep breathing exercises can help alleviate stress and potentially reduce symptom severity.

Yes, stress and emotional factors can influence diverticulitis symptoms. Stress can lead to increased inflammation in the body and affect gastrointestinal function, potentially triggering or worsening symptoms such as abdominal pain and discomfort. Practicing stress management techniques like yoga, meditation, or deep breathing exercises can help reduce stress levels and promote relaxation, which may contribute to symptom relief. Incorporating these practices into your daily routine alongside dietary modifications can support overall well-being and improve symptom management.

# Conclusion

As we conclude this comprehensive guide on managing diverticulitis, it's essential to reflect on the breadth of information and insights we've explored across the seven chapters. From understanding the intricacies of diverticular disease to practical dietary guidelines, holistic approaches, and navigating daily life with this condition, our journey has been aimed at empowering individuals with the knowledge and tools to lead healthier lives.

Diverticulitis, stemming from diverticulosis, involves inflammation of pouches in the colon. This condition, prevalent among older adults, varies in severity, from mild discomfort to acute episodes requiring medical intervention. By delving into its pathophysiology and symptomatology, we've provided a foundational understanding crucial for effective management.

A cornerstone of our discussions has been the pivotal role of diet in mitigating symptoms and preventing flare-ups. Detailed strategies for each phase—flare-up, acute, and remission—have been outlined to guide dietary choices that promote healing and digestive health. From clear liquid diets during flare-ups to gradually reintroducing fiber in remission, these dietary adjustments are pivotal in managing symptoms and enhancing quality of life.

Exploring not only what to eat but also foods to avoid has been integral. This knowledge empowers individuals to make informed dietary decisions that support their health goals, emphasizing the impact of nutrition on symptom severity and overall well-being.

Beyond dietary considerations, we've explored holistic practices that complement medical treatment. Yoga, meditation, and stress management techniques have been highlighted for their potential to reduce inflammation, alleviate stress, and foster overall wellness. These practices empower individuals to nurture their emotional, physical, and spiritual well-being, enhancing resilience in managing chronic health challenges like diverticulitis.

Practicality and integration into daily life have been recurring themes. From creating personalized meal plans and maintaining food journals to incorporating regular exercise and mindfulness practices, every suggestion has aimed to enhance feasibility and sustainability in managing diverticulitis. These practical tools are designed to support adherence to treatment plans and promote long-term health outcomes.

Throughout our exploration, we've underscored the importance of personalized medical advice and collaboration with healthcare providers. While this guide offers comprehensive insights and recommendations, individualized care remains paramount. Healthcare professionals play a crucial role in providing tailored guidance, monitoring progress, and adjusting treatment plans based on individual responses and evolving health needs.

Knowledge has been positioned as a powerful tool in managing diverticulitis. By fostering understanding of the condition, its triggers, and effective management strategies, this guide aims to empower individuals to take proactive steps toward health and well-being. Beyond managing symptoms, this empowerment encourages lifestyle choices that promote resilience, support overall health, and optimize quality of life.

In conclusion, managing diverticulitis demands a multifaceted approach integrating dietary adjustments, holistic practices, and collaborative healthcare. This guide serves as a comprehensive resource for navigating the complexities of this condition with confidence and resilience. Whether newly diagnosed or seeking additional strategies for ongoing management, the information shared here serves as a roadmap for informed decision-making and positive lifestyle changes.

Each person's journey with diverticulitis is unique, requiring personalized approaches and a commitment to self-care. Embrace the opportunity to discover what works best for you, prioritize your well-being, and remain proactive in seeking support when needed. With dedication, knowledge, and a holistic approach to wellness, individuals can effectively manage diverticulitis and embrace a fulfilling life.

Thank you for embarking on this journey toward better health and well-being with us. We extend our gratitude to all healthcare professionals, researchers, and individuals whose expertise and experiences have contributed to this guide. May this knowledge empower you to navigate diverticulitis with confidence, resilience, and optimism for a healthier future.

Here's to your continued success, vitality, and well-being!

# References

Breedvelt, J. J. F., Amanvermez, Y., Harrer, M., Karyotaki, E., Gilbody, S., Bockting, C. L. H., Cuijpers, P., & Ebert, D. D. (2019). The Effects of Meditation, Yoga, and Mindfulness on Depression, Anxiety, and Stress in Tertiary Education Students: A Meta-Analysis. *Frontiers in Psychiatry*, *10*(193). https://doi.org/10.3389/fpsyt.2019.00193

Carr, S., & Velasco, A. L. (2020). *Colon Diverticulitis*. PubMed; StatPearls Publishing. https://www.ncbi.nlm.nih.gov/books/NBK541110/

CDC. (2024, May 14). *Adult Obesity Facts*. Obesity. https://www.cdc.gov/obesity/php/data-research/adult-obesity-facts.html#:~:text=The%20prevalence%20of%20obesity%20among

Chapman MD, J. R., & Wolff MD, B. G. (2006). *Colon Diverticulosis - an overview | ScienceDirect Topics*. Www.sciencedirect.com. https://www.sciencedirect.com/topics/medicine-and-dentistry/colon-diverticulosis#:~:text=Although%20most%20people%20who%20have

https://www.facebook.com/WebMD. (2004, July 9). *Diverticular Disease*. WebMD; WebMD. https://www.webmd.com/digestive-disorders/diverticular-disease

National Institute of Diabetes and Digestive and Kidney Diseases. (2021, August). *Definition & Facts for Diverticular Disease | NIDDK*. National Institute of Diabetes and Digestive and Kidney Diseases. https://www.niddk.nih.gov/health-information/digestive-diseases/diverticulosis-diverticulitis/definition-facts

Made in the USA
Las Vegas, NV
08 May 2025

21849686R00050